I0519261

Light In The Valley

Sermons that Matter from Psalms, Prophets and Parables

George R. Estes

Parson's Porch Books

Light In The Valley: Sermons that Matter from Psalms, Prophets and Parables
ISBN: Softcover 978-1-960326-73-7
Copyright © 2024 by George R. Estes

Parson's Porch Books is an imprint of Parson's Porch *&* Company (PP*&*C) in Cleveland, Tennessee. PP*&*C is a self-funded charity which earns money by publishing books of noted authors, representing all genres. Its face and voice is **David Russell Tullock** (dtullock@parsonsporch.com).

Parson's Porch *&* Company *turns books into bread & milk* by sharing its profits with the poor.

www.parsonsporch.com

Light In The Valley

DEDICATION

For my father,

Rev. Sam R. Estes, Jr. (1919-2021)

My first and most enduring model for ministry

and

For Janie, who heard them all… almost

CONTENTS

PREFACE

The sermons in this collection, with only a few exceptions, were developed and delivered in the years I served as primary caregiver for my wife Janie, who suffered a disabling stroke in January 2017. At that time I had been retired from full-time ministry only three years. Janie was welcomed into the heavenly choir on October 8, 2022. Until that time, she was invariably my first "audience" for preaching, though never once offering a single criticism. I like to think she still listens to my sermons, and I continue sharing them with her. These messages were offered against the backdrop of the realities of life with her during her poor health, and life after her passing. The reader may notice frequent references to our biblical hope. That has sustained me through many dark hours.

No attempt has been made to update the sermons. They sometimes acknowledge the challenges of the Coronavirus pandemic, for example, and refer to other current events and personalities in the news. When working as an interim pastor or as regular pulpit supply, I typically based sermons on one of the lectionary readings for the day. These sermons are introduced with a verse or two, but a reading of the full Bible lesson preceded preaching. My practice has been to write a manuscript for every sermon but have generally sought (with trepidation) to speak without notes. I consult commentaries and other references, yet strive to find my own slant on the passages. I enjoy using a variety of Bible translations for preaching, but most texts referenced here are from the New Revised Standard Version, Revised Standard Version, or New International Version. A sensitivity to the use of pronouns, particularly with reference to God, is hereby affirmed, though I capitulate to the masculine more often than not.

It has been my privilege to preach in several congregations in the ten years since my retirement. I acknowledge with deep appreciation these that I have served most often in the time frame represented in these pages: First Presbyterian Church of Holly Springs, Mississippi; Cumberland Presbyterian Church of Germantown, Tennessee; First Presbyterian Church of Rosemark, Tennessee; and Mt. Carmel Cumberland Presbyterian Church near Somerville, Tennessee.

George R. Estes, D.Min.
Germantown, Tennessee

PSALMS

BE STILL!

Be still and now that I am God. Psalm 46:10

Recently I heard a frazzled parent say to her little girl, "Be still!" It reminded me of the days when my own children were young and seemed to know instinctively when I needed them to behave and were determined not to. I've said, "Be still!" a few times, I'm sure. I heard my parents tell me that a few times back in the day, as well. I expect most of us have some negative history with the phrase, "Be still!" But in Psalm 46 there is a different feeling associated with the imperative phrase, "Be still." Here the connotation is not a reprimand but an invitation.

Someone gave me a little devotional guide titled <u>Stillness and Strength</u> a number of years ago. It was written by a minister of the Church of England in the first quarter of the twentieth century, but its simplicity, beauty and depth seemed timeless. It taught an approach to one's prayer life that called for 'abiding realizingly in God's Presence' throughout the day, not merely in one's designated prayer time. Cultivating a continuous awareness of the Presence of God engendered a sense of peace and purpose. I passed that little book along to another person somewhere along the line, but its message has stayed with me. I thought of it again when I saw a plaque on the wall of my wife's room at Baptist Memorial Rehabilitation Center. There is a verse on the plaque from Psalm 46: "Be still and know that I am God." [verse 10] I have no doubt that many patients and family members will have occasion to reflect on those words as I have while they are in that room.

I. STILLNESS

There is, from a biblical perspective, a certain tranquility and assurance in stillness. The wonderful 23rd Psalm expresses gratitude that the Good Shepherd leads us "beside the still waters." In other words, our Lord brings us to the oasis in a dry land, a place of refuge, refreshment and restoration. God brings us to streams of living water when we are exhausted from life's many travels. Such is stillness in the Presence of God.

The prophet Elijah, despite being victorious over a hoard of idolatrous prophets, ran for his life when he heard the wicked Queen Jezebel was after him. [1 Kings 19:3] Hiding in a cave, the prophet lamented that he alone was faithful to God, and now he felt his own life was at risk. But the Lord told him to get out of the cave and stand on the mountaintop. When he did, there arose a great, destructive whirlwind, and even the rocks shook with the force of it. But the Lord was not in the wind. Then there was a mighty earthquake and the whole mountain trembled beneath the frightened prophet. But the Lord was not in the earthquake. No sooner did the tremors subside than a wildfire hurtled up the hillside. But the Lord didn't speak from the flames, either. Instead, when the tumult finally stopped, there came a still small voice, and Elijah heard it, the voice of the Lord.

Once when Jesus was in a boat with his disciples on the Sea of Galilee, he found a place in the back of the boat to take a little nap. But as sometimes happens on that body of water, a violent storm suddenly swept down from the cliffs above. Waves crashed over the bow and threatened to swamp the fishing craft. Though some of the disciples were seasoned men of the sea, they were near panic in that storm. One of them made his way back to where the Master was sleeping and, shaking his shoulders, cried: 'Don't you care that we are perishing?' But when he awoke, Jesus seemed puzzled by the disciples' fear. "Why are you afraid? Have you little faith?" Then he stood in the storm-tossed boat and rebuked the winds and waves: "Peace! Be Still!" Instantly a great calm hushed the storm, and the disciples were amazed and filled with wonder. [Mark 4:35ff]

So often our lives are characterized by a hectic pace. We seem scarcely to complete one task before feeling the pressure of another. It is no coincidence that the term multi-tasking has emerged in our lifetime. People in business refer to the "rat race," the frenzied attempt to keep up with ever-changing realities in the marketplace, to stay relevant, to fend off the competition. Teachers find it challenging to provide sufficient information in a comparatively short amount of time so that students can do well on standardized tests. Agribusiness has to maximize the time because seasonal weather can determine profitability. People in the high-tech industry are constantly tweaking new digital applications, while those in science and medicine continuously push the envelope in research and production. Churches, too, are often swept along by the desire to stay current and to adjust the spiritual thermostat accordingly. In virtually every walk of life, we are on the lookout for whatever is "new and improved." As a result, we are a generation that is easily bored, a people leery of contemplation in favor of getting something done.

This notion of stillness, then, doesn't seem to fit our contemporary way of life. It sounds archaic to Madison Avenue, nostalgic to Main Street, anachronistic to the halls of legislature. We are people on the move, aware of the adage that if you're standing still, you're falling behind.

II. WORSHIP AND STILLNESS

Our experience of worship, though, invites us to be still in a different sort of way. Yes, in our public worship services we are rather still most of the time, but that isn't what I mean. To come into the Presence of the Lord

14

is to find ourselves in a stillness that has less to do with our physical energy and more to do with the spiritual movement within. When the Lord Jesus called his disciples, he invited them to follow him, not stay put! The Gospels reveal a wandering group led by an itinerant preacher. Christ had the Twelve always on the move, but that did not undermine the quiet stillness and strength with which he led them. Though the storms of controversy waged all around him, the Lord remained the picture of serenity and peace. Never in haste, he was always ahead of others.

In his Sermon on the Mount, Christ counseled his followers to have no anxiety about anything, but to trust in the Heavenly Father for all things. [Mt 5:31-32] This is a tall order for those of us who bounce around like a pinball from one responsibility to the next. But this is surely part of the secret of knowing God in the stillness, as our Psalm suggests. Ultimately the question for us is whether or not we trust the Lord. It is that trust that wells up as the stillness of peace that passes all understanding.

There is a familiar hymn in our book that deals with this.

"Be still, my soul: the Lord is on thy side.
Bear patiently the cross of grief or pain.
Leave to thy God to order and provide,
Who through all changes faithful will remain.
Be still, my soul: thy best, thy heavenly Friend
Through thorny ways leads to a joyful end." [Kathrina von Schlegel 1752]

The stillness of the soul is not the absence of activities or the abandoning of ongoing responsibilities and challenges. Neither is it the careless indifference of those who have no agenda beyond themselves. Rather it is the experience of assurance and peace <u>in the midst of</u> the trials and turmoil of our busy lives, the awareness that our lives have a purpose within the overarching will of God.

Our Lord said, "Come unto me all you who are overburdened and I will give you rest." [Matthew 11:28] The rest of which he spoke was not the cessation of labors, if what we know of the lives of the apostles is any indicator! It was instead a rest of the soul that finds joy, purpose and peace in the service of our God.

III. KNOWLEDGE IN STILLNESS

I find it instructive that the Psalmist places this powerful verse in the context of a longer passage featuring cataclysmic episodes. The mountains shake, the earth shifts, the nations rage, kingdoms totter. God breaks the weapons of human warfare and brings desolation on a wayward world. Then this: "Be still, and know that I am God." It is the whisper of a mighty God, speaking in that still small voice that somehow is heard over the tumult all around.

Proverbs teaches that the knowledge of God is the beginning of wisdom. [Proverbs 1:7] Here the Lord speaks through the Psalmist inviting us to a knowledge of God in the stillness.

For me, the opposite of stillness is impatience. Sometimes we are impatient -- with others, with ourselves, even with God. The experience of recovering from illness tests our patience to the utmost. Perhaps that's why the medical field refers to such folks as "patients." It isn't easy to be still when our deepest yearnings and instincts are to get moving, to put the difficulty behind us, to patch things up as quickly as possible and get on with life. Of course I have been sensitized to this through my wife's illness, and am trying to guard against an unhelpful impatience as we anticipate an extended period of recovery and adjustments to our ordinary routine. There are times when life slows us down, makes us think of things in a new way, gives us a fresh perspective. What a consolation it is to know that it is in the stillness that we find a divine strength. For when things seem to us most out of control, that is when we are most keenly aware of our need of God. In this stillness, God is very real.

HOW LONG?

How long, O Lord? Will you forget me forever?
How long will you hide your face from me? Psalm 13:1

If we didn't know better, we might say the poet who penned Psalm 13 was living in 2020 instead of three thousand years ago! It's been a rough year so far, perhaps we'll all agree. The psalmist cries, "How long, O Lord? Will you forget me forever?" And we who are still struggling with the impositions and continuing threat of the Coronavirus pandemic, along with the concurrent calls for a refreshed commitment to social justice, find ourselves wondering if this unsettling time will ever end. We are doing our best to adjust to this new normal, but it's not easy.

Anyone who has dealt with a chronic illness, or faced a serious financial reversal, or been involved in a running feud with someone is personally familiar with the question "How long?" As a caregiver one realizes that some days just don't work out very well, and the care receiver may wonder how long they can endure this misfortune. The other day as I walked my dog I met a grandmother with two young children riding bikes. At a short distance away she explained that they were afraid of dogs, so I re-routed to keep away from them. Then she cried with exasperation, "And they've been out of school since March!" The implication was clear: she had just about had it!

It probably is just part of the human condition to be faced at some point with ongoing trials that leave us feeling desperate. It certainly was part of the psalmist's reality! So when the Bible lectionary suggestions for today included Psalm 13, the almost-contemporary voice of the psalmist beckoned a closer listen.

There are a couple of things to notice about this psalm even before the first verse. Like most of the psalms, this one has a superscription, a comment about the psalm's use and/or derivation. It says: "To the leader. A Psalm of David." Earlier translations rendered this: "To the Choirmaster…" These instructions and textual notes are obscure to us. But we can at least conjecture that the first part of this superscription suggests that the psalm was to be used by a choir and congregation. We know that the psalms were often sung or recited in the Temple services, and probably in individual and family devotions as well. We do the same today, because many of our hymns are inspired by the psalms.   Last Sunday a comment was made in our time together about the great hymn by Martin Luther, "A

17

Mighty Fortress Is Our God." Hymnologists tell us it was taken from Psalm 43. And the psalm we're considering today was also important in the Reformation period. It was one of 18 psalms John Calvin had set to music and included in his hymnbook for congregational use, published in 1539. However, I haven't found in our current hymnbook a hymn based on Psalm 13, though there are hosts of hymns based on the psalms. This psalm, though, candid as it is, was intended for use in congregational worship. In other words, its concerns are not just individual and personal; they are the outpouring of the people of God in worship!

The second part of that superscription warrants attention, too. It is "A Psalm of David." Bible scholars wrangle over this kind of information, but in general it is held that the Book of Psalms is an anthology developed over a long time with contributions from many writers. David certainly was one of them, though it's not likely he wrote all the poems attributed to him in this Book. Rather, it may be that he was instrumental in commissioning certain psalms to be written for worship. An example of this is from the time when King David brought the ark of the covenant to Jerusalem and ordered a psalm to be prepared for the occasion. [1 Chronicles 8:36ff] And there are psalms that are associated with David because they seem to describe events from his life. [Cf., Psalm 57, where David flees from Saul] It is remembered that David himself was a poet and musician, and his commitment to the worship life of the nation led eventually to the construction of the majestic Temple in Jerusalem during Solomon's time. So Psalm 13 may not have come directly from David's hand, but his imprint is surely upon it.

Yet the pathos and perseverance exhibited in this psalm are not confined to a single person, time or place. It could be thought of as lifting up the angst of any believing soul in the midst of suffering. There are three parts to the psalm, and we'll take a look at each of them. I refer to them as "the cry of faith," "the concern of faith," and "the confidence of faith."

1. THE CRY OF FAITH

We hear the cry of faith from that first phrase, "How long?" And it is repeated four times in two brief verses. But it is important to realize that the particular expression of impatience, heartache and anguish in the psalm can arise only in the context of belief in God. The person who does not believe in God cannot utter, "How long, <u>O Lord</u>?" Such an individual may well experience the pain and disappointment of prolonged suffering, but he or she does not cry out to God, for in their mind no God exists to hear their appeal.

Nor, I submit, is this the cry of a superficial belief in God. There are folks whose belief in God depends almost completely on their own well-being. When that is lacking or at risk, their conviction as to God's existence, or at least God's care, evaporates. The story of Job in the Old Testament reveals the kind of faith that we find in this psalm. Job was beset with one traumatic experience after another, but though he bitterly complained to God, he never faltered in his faith. 'Though he slay me,' said Job, 'yet will I trust in him.' [Job 13:15, KJV] It is one thing to maintain belief in God when life is good and all our needs are met. It is quite another to retain that faith when calamities befall us. Having said that, I can attest that some of the most powerful testimonies I have encountered over the years have been from the lips and lives of persons who endured great suffering. No superficial faith there!

From the depths of despair, the psalmist cries out to God. There seems to be no end to his ordeal. So isolated and aggrieved is he that he thinks perhaps God has forgotten him, or that God is actually hiding from him. Maybe we've had times in our own lives when we have thought something like that. Someone has said there are times when we wear our hurts as well as our hearts on our sleeve! That's when the pain and sorrow seem too much to bear. Yet the person of faith cries out to <u>God</u>, even from that place of deep suffering. It reminds us, doesn't it, of the cry of faith we have so often heard from the Garden of Gethsemane. 'If it be your will, let this cup pass from me. Nevertheless, not my will but yours be done!' [Luke 42:22] And from the Cross we hear our Savior's parched voice, quoting Psalm 22: 'My God, my God, why have you forsaken me?' This sense of being alone in the throes of agony still lays claim to the reality and power of God! It is a cry of faith.

What a blessing it is that at least most of the time we do not venture near this level of pain and suffering. But what an assurance it is, also, that when we must endure long suffering, we can lift up the cry of faith just as this psalm does. The individual believer and the believing congregation can ask, "How long, O Lord?" For this is a cry of faith.

2. THE CONCERN OF FAITH

We detect in this psalm, also, the concern of faith. Surrounded by nations whose gods were not the Lord, Israel was continually aware of the scorn of its neighbors from a purely religious perspective. The general feeling of the time was that a people's deity wasn't worth much if they suffered hardship or were defeated in battle. In that case the conqueror's gods were considered mightier than those of the vanquished. But Israel's faith in the Lord was different. They came to realize that while God was often victorious over their enemies in their behalf, there were also those occasions when the Lord exercised judgment over his people by allowing them to fall victim to the surrounding peoples. But the concern of faith

19

expressed in this psalm is the worry that Israel's enemies might gloat over their misfortune, might feel as if their deities were greater than Yahweh!

Again, the agnostic or atheist has no such concern. Even the erstwhile believer isn't bothered much by what others think of the true God. For such a one it's 'live and let live,' 'you go to your church I'll go to mine.' It doesn't really make a difference. Someone else may refuse to admit the possibility that enemies of genuine faith do exist. But the people of ancient Israel labored under no such misconception. Today's people of faith shouldn't, either.

Enemies are real. But they aren't really the "straw men" we Christians often put up – atheists and agnostics, for example! No, the real enemies of faith today are those whose belief in God is not transformative enough to challenge their inappropriate attitudes and behaviors, whose belief system is more about confirming their own opinions than hearkening to the Word of God. When people who do believe in God come across as hypocritical, hyper-judgmental, racist, greedy, or morally sub-par, then the secular community sees that as proof enough that God either doesn't exist or is powerless to do anything about God's own people! We're reminded of that comic strip philosopher Pogo who said, 'We have met the enemy and he is us!' (Walt Kelly, paraphrasing naval officer Oliver Hazard Perry, 1813)

The concern of faith in this psalm reminds us not only of outside threats, but also the enemies within, those tendencies we have to give in to our lesser selves when things get rough. Perhaps we are in such a time now.

3. THE CONFIDENCE OF FAITH

But that's not where the psalm ends. Almost out of the blue the final two verses show us the confidence of faith. 'I trusted in your steadfast love, Lord, and my heart shall rejoice in your salvation, because you have blessed me so!' (My own paraphrase!) There are several important tenses in this affirmation. There's the past tense: I trusted your steadfast love, Lord. There's the future tense: My heart shall rejoice in your salvation. And there is the ongoing sense of being continually blessed. It's in this stanza of the psalm that we are convinced that the writer behind all the questioning, the ranting and the worry is indeed a person of faith. The psalmist finds hope in the midst of the difficulty, counts on God when all looks bleak, affirms God's blessings when no one else would find any. So often I have heard someone say, 'I'm so blessed, I can't afford to complain.' Frequently that comment comes from a person who is having a pretty tough go. For our trust in God is not confined to our present circumstances, be they good or ill. We rejoice not that all things are well, but that God is really God, and that God really cares!

20

So in this continuing community limbo, though we have no answer to our question of "how long," we do have the conviction that we may depend on the grace of God to see us through. By the way, there are at least a couple of times in Scripture when the <u>Lord</u> asks, "How long?" One of those was when Jesus returned from the Mount of Transfiguration only to find that his disciples down below had been unable to help a distraught father whose son was quite ill. 'How long must I put up with this unbelieving generation?' he wondered. [Matthew 17:17] Now there's a sobering thought!

A BIG LITTLE WORD

All the earth worships you; they sing praises to your name. Selah. Psalm 66:4

A word doesn't have to be big to be potent. The little word "virus," for example, had become almost completely associated with a mischievous or malicious bug in your computer until a couple of months ago, when suddenly it became a frightening healthcare threat again. Take the word "zoom." It had always been a comic book sound effect, but now it's our way of communicating from home to home and heart to heart! Atom is another tiny word packed with power. And what about small words like pain, or joy, or egg? The Bible is full of big little words. In fact, if you subtract the proper names from Scripture, it's largely composed of small words, and many of them bear great impact! Faith, hope and love come to mind, along with the biggest little word of all: God.

There's a little word in the Psalms that stumps even the most diligent Bible scholars. It usually appears in italics after a paragraph. The word is "Selah," which appears three times in the Sixty-sixth Psalm considered today. It actually occurs seventy-one times in the Psalms, but only three other times in the Bible, all in the third chapter of Habakkuk. [verses 3, 9, 13] Somewhere along the line you may have been advised, as I was, not to read this word aloud when you come to it in the text. It was thought to be silent instruction to the musicians, sort of like a rest in a musical score. But no one really knows what the ancient Hebrew word signified. Some suggestions have been put forward, naturally. It could be, for instance, a break for an instrumental interlude, an opportunity for the choir to catch a breath, or it might have been a choral response similar to "amen," meaning "so be it."

Authorities agree that it was a liturgical note indicating a pause of some kind, as if to emphasize the preceding words. In this case, it would connote something like "Stop and Listen!" Viewed that way, it's a power word, a big little word! That's the way I'm thinking about it anyhow as we reflect on this Sixty-sixth Psalm. There's a sense in which we have been in a pause state for quite a while! Have we also taken this time as an opportunity to "Stop and Listen?"

The presence of this little word "Selah" in our text today reminds us to pause and consider what the hymn is about. It is a call to worship, an invitation to praise God. The Psalmist beckons, first, the whole earth to sing out God's praise. Then God's people are to join the song. And the Psalm concludes with a personal affirmation and praise for God's steadfast love.

1. MAKE A JOYFUL NOISE TO GOD, ALL THE EARTH

The modern lifestyle doesn't take much notice of the natural world. We whizz by it at seventy miles an hour – and that's only on land. Once we get above the clouds, jetting away, the patchwork of land below seems almost unreal. We often do look forward to vacations at the beach, in the mountains, or at the fishing stream. These are meaningful, relaxing times for us because they allow us the space and time to get in touch with our natural surroundings once more. Invariably we are impressed with nature's beauty and we momentarily regret having to leave it all to return to our brick and asphalt routine. The world's population is increasingly compressed into cities, and one result is the loss of contact with nature, and to an extent, nature's God.

The Psalms are full of references about nature extolling the greatness of God. 'When I consider the heavens, the work of your hands, what are human beings that you are mindful of them?' [Psalm 8:3] And again, 'O Lord, how manifold are your works! In wisdom you have made them all; the earth is full of your creatures.' [Psalm 104:24] 'The Lord is king! Let the earth rejoice… The heavens proclaim his righteousness.' [Psalm 97:1, 6] 'The heavens are telling the glory of God; and the firmament proclaims his handiwork.' [Psalm 19:1]

The Hebrew people lived close to the land, even though it was often admittedly a harsh land. They were more familiar with the night sky than most of us, because their only illumination after sunset was a candle, a flickering oil lamp, a torch, or moonlight! They were attuned to the passing of seasons as only an agrarian society can be. For them planting and harvest were natural realities that spoke profoundly of spiritual truth. Water was precious in an arid climate, and so it too came to symbolize spiritual cleansing and thirst quenching. Mountains lifted the eye and thus the spirit to the heavens. The people of Bible times knew something of animals, both domesticated and feral. So the Psalmist acknowledges what seems abundantly evident to him, that all the earth makes joyous noise to the Lord's wondrous power and creativity.

Ours is a noisy world, too. But so often the noise around us gives no attention to the praise of God. It will be up to us, in our Selah moments, to hear the prayer in a bubbling brook, the song in the rustle of leaves, the proclamation in the thunderclap. It is the person of faith who is given grace to notice the divine artistry in the seeming chaos of the animal kingdom, or to sense a parable of the mighty power of God when, with just a flick of a switch, a light comes on in our room. It will take a moment's reflection to observe the healing hand of God as that masked Coronavirus survivor rolls through the hospital corridor to the cheers of the medical staff! Here in our own time and circumstances, the Psalmist reminds us, and all the earth, to give God glorious praise. "Stop and Listen!"

2. BLESS OUR GOD, O PEOPLES

While there is a kind of praise of the Creator in the natural world, the Psalmist is quick to point out the need for the peoples of earth to acknowledge God, too. "Bless our God, O peoples," the Psalmist cries. Scripture consistently affirms that God is engaged in the affairs of nations and peoples. The prophet Amos, for instance, began his work with a countdown of the transgressions of the great cities and nations of the Mideast: Damascus, Tyre, Moab. These led inexorably to the Lord's indictment of Israel and Judah, the people who had been chosen for a testimony to God's power, glory and goodness, but who had failed in their mission. [Amos 1-3] Isaiah declared the Persian ruler Cyrus to be the Lord's anointed, that is, he (though not an Israelite) would be the vessel God would use to deliver his people. [Isaiah 45:1] In other words, these prophetic utterings affirm God is sovereign over all peoples, not just the people of Israel, and not just the people of the church in our day. All humanity is urged to acknowledge the Creator God. But particularly those who marked their sacred history by the transforming events of the Exodus, the possession of the Promised Land, the deliverance from Babylonian captivity. And for us Christians, especially, it is our privilege and obligation to praise God for our redemption from sin and death through the death and resurrection of Jesus Christ.

Few nations today appear to acknowledge the Lord in the fashion of the big little word "Selah." We are in a multi-cultural world where it is abundantly clear we must cultivate not only a tolerance of, but an appreciation for the variety of religious and political worldviews. Without this, we are doomed to incessant warfare and terrorism.

It may be that we can relate to the Psalmist's note that today we are being tested as silver is tried. [verse 10] The pandemic has forced us to think globally as well as locally. It has re-routed our daily lives in ways none of us could have imagined only a short time ago. As so many TV ads declare, we are in this together. At the same time, we people of biblical faith recognize that God is Lord of all, whether all may acknowledge God or not. We are compelled to find ways of cooperative living in this fractured world. A place to start is with that big little word which calls us to "Stop and Listen!"

24

3. BLESSED BE GOD, WHO HAS LISTENED TO MY PRAYER

Our psalm doesn't end with affirming creation's praise of God, nor even with the opportunity for the nations to join that praise. No, despite the universal and even cosmic implications of this psalm, there is another point to consider. Because for the psalmist, the relationship with God is personal! God has listened to the singer's prayer, God has accepted the psalmist's acts of worship, God has never ceased showing steadfast love to the one who tagged "Selah" after his verses!

Our Selah moment reminds us that God loves us every one. We come to God empty handed, we come in spiritual tatters, we come burdened with cares and concerns, freighted with the repercussions of our misdeeds, acutely aware of our shortcomings. But toward the penitent our God is gracious, slow to anger, full of steadfast love, and abundantly pardons those who trust in him. [Psalm 145:8] We know this because of another big little word.

In his great hymn the Reformer Martin Luther has an intriguing line:

"The prince of darkness grim – We tremble not for him;
His rage we can endure, For lo! his doom is sure,
One little word shall fell him."

What is that one little word, do you think? I believe it is the Word that was with God from the beginning, the Word through whom all creation was made and exists. [John 1:1ff] It is a little word that means 'God will save his people.' [Matthew 1:21] It is a name, really, a name that evokes our Selah praises as no other. 'For God has given him a name above all others, that at the name of Jesus, every knee should bend in heaven and on earth, and every tongue confess that Jesus Christ is Lord, to the glory of God the Father.' [Philippians 2:10-11] Selah!

25

A SPECIAL WISDOM

The fear of the Lord is the beginning of wisdom;
all those who practice it have a good understanding.
His praise endures forever. Psalm 111:10

"Where is the one who is wise? Where is the scribe? Where is the
debater of this age? Has not God made foolish the wisdom of the
world? ... For God's foolishness is wiser than human wisdom, and
God's weakness is stronger than human strength." 1 Corinthians
1:20, 25

Sometimes I think I must have wasted a lot of time in school, especially when I remember some of the bonehead moves I've made over the years. Education is supposed to make us smarter, equip us for making good decisions, prepare us for the real world. In my case, I hope it helped, because there's no telling how much more I might have goofed up without it! Church and Sunday school, further, are generally regarded as constructive for a person's spiritual understanding and moral compass. Again, without that exposure I don't relish the thought of how I might have done. But I can't blame the educational system or the church for any misjudgments or failings. Those have been all my own! I mention this because one would think that having reached retirement years, I could reasonably expect to have gained some wisdom along the way. That's the way we usually think of wisdom, isn't it? It comes with age, experience and gray hair. Unfortunately, at times I've had reason to question this popular notion!

One of the recurring sub-themes in our Scripture lessons so far this year has been the notion of wisdom. There were the "wise men" from the East who visited the Christ Child and presented their gifts of gold, frankincense and myrrh. And being wise, they skirted wicked King Herod's designs when they headed home. Then we read of the young lad Jesus in the Temple at age twelve. Following that experience, the Gospel writer tells us Jesus grew in wisdom and in stature and in favor with God and man. [Luke 2:52] Then we considered the story of the child Samuel in the shrine at Shiloh under the tutelage of the old priest Eli. We read that he too grew in wisdom and in stature. [1 Samuel 2:26] This emphasis on the wisdom of these youngsters surprises us a bit, because, again, our typical perspective is that wisdom comes only with age and experience.

You may remember that when Ronald Reagan, at age 73, was running for President against the younger Walter Mondale, Reagan quipped, "I am not going to exploit, for political purposes, my opponent's youth and inexperience." This drew laughter from Mondale and the rest of the country.

Psalm 111, which was a lectionary suggestion for today, includes a famous verse: "The fear of the Lord is the beginning of wisdom." [Psalm 111:10] That verse sticks in the memory so well that we assume it must be written on practically every page of the Bible! But no, we actually can find only one other instance of this exact wording: Proverbs 9:10. There are plenty of other verses that say virtually the same thing, though. Proverbs 1:7 says, "The fear of the Lord is the beginning of knowledge." That's mighty close. In the book of Job the Lord himself says: "Truly, the fear of the Lord, that is wisdom." [Job 28:28] Recently I was asked to write Sunday school lessons from two of the Bible's Wisdom books, Job and Ecclesiastes. So I've been giving a lot of thought to this idea of wisdom in Scripture, and in particular the wisdom arising from one's relationship to God. In reverence and obedience to God, these passages affirm, there is the potential for human beings to gain special wisdom.

There is a different take on wisdom in our reading from First Corinthians, though. There the apostle Paul, writing to the Greek Corinthians who we may assume knew something about the philosophers of their heritage, contrasts the wisdom of this world with the wisdom of God. These new Christians were familiar with the teachings of Socrates, Plato and other luminaries of their history. But now they had been given, through Paul's ministry, a new perspective on wisdom. It was a level of wisdom that was not available to the greatest thinkers of their tradition. For that matter, it was wisdom unparalleled in Paul's Jewish heritage, too. In the Hebrew Scriptures, there was none wiser than King Solomon. His wisdom was heralded far and wide. The Queen of Sheba declared his imminence. Yet Jesus declared "a greater than Solomon is here." [Matthew 12:42] In fact, Paul conceded, the wisdom of God of which he spoke would seem outrageous and ridiculous to the most learned in the Greek and Jewish society of the day. "We proclaim Christ crucified," said Paul, "a stumbling block to Jews and foolishness to Gentiles." But to those who are called, he went on, "Christ the power of God and the wisdom of God." [1 Corinthians 1:24]

1. JESUS EMBODIED THE WISDOM AND POWER OF GOD

Jesus the Messiah embodied the wisdom and power of God. No reading of the four Gospels can miss that affirmation. Jesus revealed divine wisdom in his teachings. The Sermon on the Mount offered an unprecedented way of living for God. The Parables illustrated the foibles of human beings, but also the righteousness and grace of Almighty God. Christ's declaration of the immediacy of the kingdom of God, his capacity to bring the Scriptures to light in his own Person, his ability to know the hearts and minds of the people he met all point to a matchless wisdom. When the religious leaders heard him, they were amazed at his wisdom. That was the case when he was still a boy in the Jerusalem Temple, and it was even more evident when he taught as an adult. In the first chapter of Mark we are told that when he taught in the synagogue at Capernaum, "they were astounded at his teaching, for he taught them as one having authority, and not as the scribes." [Mark 1:22]

2. WHAT GAVE JESUS HIS WISDOM?

What was it that gave Jesus his unusual wisdom? Was it just a natural intellect, the confluence of neurons in a well-developed brain? I once heard Jesus referred to as a genius, but that idea seemed completely off to me. Genius implies a level of thought that is a cut above – maybe several cuts in the case of a savant -- the brightest of us. That's not the way I see the mind of Christ, though. I don't doubt that as a youngster Jesus was a star pupil in the synagogue school at Nazareth. No doubt there were other children in the class who excelled, but no one else had his level of understanding. But it wasn't the fairly ordinary teaching of school that provided the wisdom we see in Christ. The Gospel evidence suggests that Jesus used at least three languages: Aramaic, the common language of the region where he lived; Hebrew, the language of the sacred scrolls from which he read in Nazareth; and Greek or Latin, the language Pontius Pilate may have used to interrogate him. Yet this linguistic knowledge would not have been all that unusual in that day, so it wasn't this that set him apart. And surely he benefited from the tradecraft he learned in the carpenter's shop, but that was not the key to his wisdom, either. I expect that in Nazareth as elsewhere there were deeply devout people, Pharisees and elders, who would have urged the young Jesus to identify with their particular group, But he remained independent of them all, for they were not the source of his wisdom. It wasn't advanced age, either, that provided Jesus' wisdom. Luke tells us he was about thirty years old when he began his ministry. [Luke 3:23] Interestingly, when he declared that 'Abraham rejoiced to see his day,' his detractors noted that he was 'not yet fifty years old.' [John 8:58] We know that our Lord's ministry lasted approximately three years, so by any reckoning he was still a young man when he stood in chains before Pontius Pilate. We must conclude that his special wisdom was not simply the intellect of a brilliant person, nor was it derived from age and experience, but it was the eternal Word of God he embodied. [John 1:14]

Jesus revealed the power of God in such miracles as calming the storm at sea, walking on water, changing water to wine, and feeding multitudes. He demonstrated divine authority by casting out evil spirits, healing all kinds of diseases, driving the moneychangers from the Temple, and raising the dead. Where did this power come from? There were many religious teachers in his day, but none taught with the level of authority he possessed, none exhibited the supernatural abilities that characterized Jesus' ministry. At the same time, he refused to use that power for personal advancement, as the account of his temptation in the wilderness underscores. [e.g., Matthew 4:3-11] He came into the world to do the will of the heavenly Father, to do the works of the One who had sent him -- nothing else. [John 6:38] His power was not the physical strength of a Samson or David. It was not the mental acumen of an Einstein. We conclude, then, that he manifested the power of God in his mighty deeds because he embodied the eternal Word. In him, says Scripture, the 'fullness of God was pleased to dwell.' [Colossians 1:19]

3. THE WISDOM AND POWER OF GOD

Jesus Christ was the power and wisdom of God Incarnate. It wasn't a matter of his having attained an age that would qualify him for wisdom in the sense of wide personal experience. It wasn't as if he could arm-wrestle someone like the muscled Peter to a standstill, though perhaps he could have. His power and wisdom were unmistakable signs of his unique Personhood -- as the Nicene Creed puts it, Very God of Very God, yet Incarnate, fully human. And this was made known in the most unlikely way: Jesus was crucified, suffering the ignoble agony and execution of a common criminal. Then he was raised again from the dead!

Paul knew that not everyone could discern this truth, that Jesus was the embodiment of the wisdom and power of God. A cadre of influential people refused to acknowledge it during Jesus' public ministry, and they joined forces to put him to death. Years afterward there were still enemies of Christ whom Paul and the other apostles encountered. So as obvious as it may seem to us who treasure the stories of the Gospels, and who fashion our theological perspectives on the teachings of Paul and Peter and the rest, the wisdom and power of God in Christ continues to be a bone of contention in the world. Many people today are unpersuaded by the Biblical witness, unmoved by the evidence of twenty-one centuries of God's faithful people following the footsteps of the Master. The wisdom of God as presented in the gospel to them seems foolish, the power of God seems weak. They prefer other kinds of wisdom, other kinds of strength. And it doesn't matter if they are young or old, the wisdom they think most highly of is their own opinion. The power they rely on is the power of the bank account, or political clout, or military might.

Yet it is still true today as it was for those people of Corinth long ago, "to those who are the called," Christ is the power and wisdom of God.

THE VALLEY OF THE SHADOW

Even though I walk through the valley of the shadow of death, I fear no evil. Psalm 23:4

He (Paul) lived there two whole years at his own expense and welcomed all who came to him, proclaiming the kingdom of God and teaching about the Lord Jesus Christ with all boldness and without hindrance. Acts 28:30

When you stroll along in the late afternoon, you have a companion who keeps perfect step with you. Your shadow! We are so accustomed to it that we hardly notice it at all. But children are often amused to see how long their shadow is. We think of that fanciful tune, *"Me and My Shadow"* popularized by Judy Garland, Frank Sinatra, Sammy Davis Jr. and others. Trees have shadows, too. We call it shade. In the hot months the shade is a welcome relief from the scorching sun. That was especially helpful to travelers in Bible times who lived in arid climes and often had to walk from place to place. The shadow of a rock, or the overhang of a cliff, could offer silent refuge in a region where there were few trees. The hymnwriter picked up that idea in this line: "The shadow of a mighty Rock within a weary land." [*Beneath the Cross of Jesus*, Elizabeth C. Clephane; Cf., Isaiah 32:2] Scripture, speaking of the assurance and shelter God provides the faithful, refers to the 'shadow of God's wings,' or the protective 'shadow of his hand.' [Psalm 63:1; Isaiah 49:2] A few weeks ago we made note of the fact that people in Jerusalem brought their sick to be healed by the apostle Peter, just in the hope that his shadow might fall on them! [Acts 5:15] And the Letters to the Colossians and Hebrews alluded to the practices of Jewish temple and religious life as a 'shadow of things to come,' that is, a prefiguring of the matchless reign of Christ. [Colossians 2:17; Hebrews 8:5] So there is a positive connotation to the notion of shadow. But there's another side to it, too, and we find it expressed in the Twenty-third Psalm.

1. THE VALLEY OF THE SHADOW

Through the years I have drawn great hope and consolation from the Twenty-third Psalm, as you may have as well. Often I have recited it at the funeral services of friends and loved ones, and have called it to mind in moments of stress and concern. In particular, verse four of the Psalm has brought solace in times of sorrow. "Yea, though I walk through the valley of the shadow of death, I will fear no evil: for thou art with me; thy rod and thy staff, they comfort me." So reads the text in the beautiful King James Version. Typically I have interpreted that verse as referring to the experience of physical death.

Certainly the danger of physical harm is represented in the Psalm. For the shepherd in Bible times who guided a flock had to be vigilant, especially going through narrow passages where predators might lurk, or rocks might slide. Sudden, violent death was an imminent threat in the mountain passes, not only for the sheep but for the shepherd as well. You recall that when the shepherd boy David went out against the giant Goliath he noted that he had fought lion and bear defending the flock. [1 Samuel 17:36] He could easily have lost his own life in defense of the sheep. So the Psalm -- perhaps the work of a young shepherd-musician named David wandering over the hills of Palestine -- clearly expresses concern for the reality of one's death. It is a profound and personal image, calling to mind the words of that old spiritual: "You gotta walk that lonesome valley, You gotta walk it by yourself. Oh, nobody else can walk it for you, You gotta walk it by yourself."

2. A DIFFERENT VIEW OF THE SHADOW

Recently, though, I have reflected on this valley of the shadow of death in a different way, and I share this with you wondering if you have considered it. I am thinking now of a similar but somewhat less obvious approach to this verse. Death itself often sheds a pretty long shadow! Please excuse me for making a personal reference for a moment. In a manner of speaking, I have been living in the shadow of death for some time, because my wife Janie suffered a stroke five years and nine months ago, and thus began a process of physical disability and decline that ended with her death last week. It seems to me that the phrase "the valley of the shadow of death" could refer not only to one's own encounter with danger and potential demise, but is just as pertinent to the heartache and challenges associated with the dying of a loved one. Those who have served as caregivers in such circumstances know what it is to walk in the shadows of that valley. That shadow deepens in the folds of grief at the end of the loved one's journey.

A friend and I were talking about this the other day when he told me that as a youngster of nine his mother passed away after a lengthy illness. He remembered that he went into his mother's bedroom to be with her often, but that when he left to go outside and play, everything seemed much brighter. It was as if he stepped from the shadows into the sunlight. That reminded me of the passage of Scripture which affirms that when we come to faith in Christ, we are a 'chosen people, and God has brought us out of darkness into his marvelous light.' [1 Peter 2:9]

31

3. JESUS, PAUL AND THE SHADOW

Our Lord Jesus passed through the shadow of death for our sakes. We can't help thinking, though, that there were others in the shadow of the Cross that day: Mary his mother, a couple other women, John the disciple, and the centurion who cried out, "Surely, this man was the son of God." [Mark 15:39] No darkness had ever been so dark as when Jesus died. No shadow of death had ever been so stultifying, profound and frightening as the one falling over those who quivered at the foot of the Cross. Yet there had been moments foreshadowing that one, hadn't there? The Master had told his disciples on more than one occasion that he must suffer death, and then rise on the third day. [Cf, Mark 8:31] On that first Good Friday, though, the shadow of death was impenetrable.

Now let me shift our attention from that scene at Calvary to the final chapter of Acts. For the last few months we have tracked the writings of Doctor Luke in the Third Gospel and the Acts of the Apostles. When we come to the twenty-eighth chapter of Acts, the end of the book, we are surprised to see that a crowd of Christians was ready to greet Paul from the ship and escort him into the Imperial City. [Acts 28:15] It is a dim reflection of that day when a solitary figure rode into the city of Jerusalem on a donkey amid the songs and shouts of followers! Paul was a Roman prisoner, but he was clearly no ordinary criminal. Even the Roman officials and Praetorian Guard realized this. So he was permitted to live in a dwelling of his own -- at his own expense of course -- under house arrest, with a guard posted at the door. We are told that he sent word to the local leaders of the Jewish community to come so he could explain to them the charges that had been brought against him in Jerusalem, and also to share the good news of Christ with them. Visitors came and went at will, and Paul was very effective in leading people to Christ. But then Luke concludes with the observation that Paul lived there two years and welcomed all who came to him, proclaiming the kingdom of God and teaching about the Lord Jesus Christ without hindrance. [Acts 28:30] But that's it! Nothing more. One would think that after spending all this time rehearsing Paul's missionary endeavors, his tribulations in various court proceedings, his difficult journey to Rome, and his date with the emperor that Luke would at least tell us how it turned out. No.

From his own letters we can detect that Paul underwent at least two trials at the Roman court, whether with the emperor or not we cannot know. In Second Timothy we learn that toward the end of his imprisonment Paul was alone – except for Luke. [2 Timothy 4:11] Reliable tradition has it that the result of his second trial was Paul's execution in about 60 AD during the reign of Nero, a couple years before the harshest persecution of Christians began. The apostle Peter is thought to have been

32

in Rome during this time as well. But Luke says nothing of this. We have only the hints of the prophetic predictions Paul heard on the way to Jerusalem as to what his ultimate fate might be. But the shadow of death hung over the apostle throughout his ministry, and particularly in those last few years.

Luke says nothing about Paul's death, I expect, because he had achieved his purpose in writing. He wanted to tell the story of the developing church from Jerusalem to the city of Rome, representing the empire itself. He did not give us details of Paul's end because he wasn't really writing a biography of Paul or Peter or anyone else. He was telling the story of the spread of the Good News of Christ throughout the Roman world of the time. Many people would lose their lives in service to the gospel, including the apostles. But the shadow of death was not the last word! It was that the gospel was proclaimed "with all boldness and without hindrance."

There was no darkness like that first Good Friday. But from that darkness there came the light of Easter! Paul knew this without question. He had seen the Light, literally.

So when we walk through that dark valley ourselves, or with someone we love, we fear no evil because the Lord is with us. His staff guides us, his rod protects us. He brings us to his house to dwell with him forever!

THE RIGHT WORD

Blessed are those whose ways are blameless, who walk according to the law of the Lord. Psalm 119:1

Some of you, I expect, have written a poem or two. And if you have, then you know how challenging it can be to find an appropriate word to express your thought while at the same time fitting it into the rhyme scheme or rhythm of the verse. Free verse, of course, has no such limitation, which may explain its popularity! But songwriters and composers of traditional poems know the discipline of conforming language to meter and sound. I mention this because when we commence a study of Psalm 119 we are astounded by the linguistic expertise of the poet-psalmist. Oh, wait, that may not be obvious in our English Bibles. But a glance at a Bible commentary, or a careful notice of the psalm in the King James Version or NIV showing strange characters over its divisions, will reveal a detail of the psalm's composition that is staggering.

There are one hundred seventy-six verses in Psalm 119, the longest in the Psalter, indeed the longest chapter in the entire Bible. But that isn't its only unique characteristic. The psalm is divided into twenty-two strophes, or stanzas, with eight lines each. Not to get too technical, but if we were looking at our hymnbook, we would think of a strophe as a verse to be sung. What is interesting, though, is that each strophe of this psalm begins with a letter of the Hebrew alphabet – the <u>aleph beth</u>, it is called, after its first two letters. There are twenty-two letters in the Hebrew <u>aleph beth</u>, and this psalm's strophes follow them consecutively. So it's an acrostic poem -- not the only one in the Bible, but surely the most impressive. And that's not all. Every line of the first strophe, all eight of them, begins with the first letter of the alphabet, the aleph. The same is true of the second strophe with the second letter, and then the third, all the way to the end. (By the way, those strange looking characters between the divisions of the psalm are actually the letters of the Hebrew alphabet.) So if you've ever puzzled over how to find a rhyme for that special word in your poem, or how to substitute one word for another to fit the meter, you can imagine what a literary feat Psalm 119 really is!

Try composing a poem in which each line begins with a letter of the English alphabet, A to Z. The mystery novelist Sue Grafton has a series of books whose titles begin with a letter of the alphabet, a terrific plan for the series but not an easy one to pull off, I'm sure. Sadly, she died in 2017 before completing the novel for Z. I just read the one for Y, titled <u>Yesterday</u>, this past week.

The linguistic structure of Psalm 119 challenges me particularly because in recent weeks I have resumed a study of Biblical Hebrew, an enterprise that unfortunately I have not kept up since my seminary days. I've had to start at the beginning, with the aleph beth, the ABCs so to speak. And I've noticed – surprise, surprise -- that it's even more difficult to learn now than it was fifty-odd years ago!

When you read Psalm 119, it may seem repetitious and monotonous. Some of the same ideas appear over and over, expressed just a little differently. Modern readers may not see the need for such an emphasis, but clearly the psalmist wanted to underscore the main idea of his poem: the perfection, beauty and power of God's word -- also referred to as God's law. There are several memorable verses to be gleaned from this psalm. It's here, for instance, that we have the wonderful verse: 'Your word is a lamp to my feet, and a light to my path.' [119:65] Another familiar phrase from this psalm is, 'Open my eyes, that I may see,' a line that is captured in one of our favorite Christian hymns. [119:18; Hymn by Clara H. Scott] Yet another great verse says, 'Your word, Lord, is eternal,' and again, 'The earth is filled with your love, O Lord.' [119:89; 65] We find deep consolation in this affirmation: 'Great peace have those who love your law, and nothing can make them stumble.' [119:165] This morning, though, let me invite you to focus on those first few verses of the psalm, the aleph stanza.

1. BLESSED ARE THOSE WHO WALK
ACCORDING TO GOD'S LAW

The first couple of verses extol the person who manages to faithfully follow the Lord's commands, the one who is blameless before the Lord. Well, yeah. That would be great, Mr. Psalmist, but who do you have in mind? Let's allow that question to dangle just a minute.

The psalms often point us toward faithfulness to God, don't they? The very first psalm says, 'Blessed is the one who does not walk in step with the wicked, whose delight is in the law of the Lord.' [1:1] But the problem, as Psalm 12 points out right away, is that 'no one is faithful anymore.' [12:1] And that is the perspective we have from the apostle Paul, too. Quoting from the Hebrew Bible, the only Scriptures he knew at the time, he said: 'There is no one righteous, not even one; there is no one who understands; there is no one who seeks God.' [Romans 3:10, citing Psalm 14:3] For Paul, and the rest of the New Testament writers, 'all have sinned and fall short of the glory of God.' [Romans 3:23]

So if Scripture declares unequivocally that no one is without sin, why does this psalm start out by praising someone who is? There are at least a couple of responses to this matter. The first is that while we all fail to live up to the divine expectation of faithfulness to God's way, it nevertheless remains a goal to work toward, a standard by which we may measure our walk with God. We know we are prone to sin, and that without God's grace we would be hopeless. But we also know that through the Spirit of the living God, we who trust in Christ may grow in his grace and strive to become "more like the Master," as another hymn says it. (Charles H. Gabriel)

In the time this psalm was written, the Messiah had not yet been revealed. There was the belief that if one tried hard enough, he or she could fully obey the laws of God. That proved not to be the case, of course, but there was that hope and belief. No doubt there were some who thought they had had achieved such perfection. We remember the story of the rich young ruler who claimed to Jesus that he had perfectly kept the law of God since his youth. Yet he knew something was missing. Jesus knew it, too. [Matthew 19:15-30] We remember, too, that Paul himself acknowledged that as to the law, he had been blameless, even as a persecutor of the church. [Philippians 3:6]

Evidently the psalmist was aware of some folks who were similarly faithful in their observance of the divine law. They were known to walk according to God's ways, and were admired for it. They sought to keep the Lord's statutes with all their heart. And so they were blessed. We cannot refrain from mentioning that this word "blessed" is associated forever with our Lord's Beatitudes. There, though, it's not a matter of perfectly adhering to the divine law but rather manifesting the characteristics of a follower of Jesus. Blessed are the poor in spirit, the meek, those who mourn, those who hunger and thirst after righteousness, and so on. [Matthew 5:1ff] But the psalmist points to the possibility, at least, of living a righteous, Godly life, and he calls that state blessed.

There is another way of to think about this psalm's viewpoint, though. When we asked who the psalmist might be referring to, who would actually live up to the righteousness God expects, only one name came to mind, right? Jesus Christ! I don't know if the psalm was intended to be prophetic, but it certainly is! For in Jesus Christ we have the fulfillment of the divine law. [Matthew 5:17-20] He was tempted as we are, yet without sin. [Hebrews 4:15]

2. OH, THAT <u>MY</u> WAYS WERE SO STEADFAST

We notice the psalmist's humility in these verses. "Oh, that <u>my</u> ways were steadfast in obeying your decrees!" If the author knew of some whose faithfulness was exemplary, he didn't consider himself in the same light. He wished for that level of righteousness, would strive for it even, but he could not attain it. Doesn't this remind us again of the apostle Paul's confession that the good he wants to do, he often fails in, and the evil he has no desire to do is what he ends up doing? [Romans 7:19] This is the dilemma we often face as people of faith. Our desire is to serve the Lord faithfully, to live according to the will of God as revealed in Scripture and exemplified in Jesus. But as the Lord once said of Peter, 'The spirit is willing, but the flesh is weak.' [Matthew 26:41]

It is this realization that convinces us of the need for grace in our Christian lives. Try as we might, we cannot achieve moral, ethical and spiritual perfection, as revealed in the divine law. Though we are committed disciples of Jesus, that 'old self' (as Paul put it) still lingers within, causing the unbidden thought, the hurtful word, the deceitful act, the careless indifference. We want to be more steadfast in our walk with God, but our feet too often stray off the narrow way.

Yet we are not left in this dismal quandary! When the apostle cried out 'Who will deliver me from this wretched body of sin and death?' he answered himself right away, "Thanks be to God, who delivers me through Jesus Christ our Lord!" [Romans 7:24-25] So in this psalm, composed centuries before the time of Paul, we hear a similar shout of acclamation!

3. I WILL PRAISE YOU WITH AN UPRIGHT HEART

Lifted from the darkness of his own weakness and shortcomings, the psalmist knows his hope is in the Lord alone. 'I will praise you with an upright heart, and obey your decrees; do not utterly forsake me – and I believe and hope and pray that you won't!' From the confession of sin to a joyous acceptance of grace, that is the posture of the one who believes in Christ. For Jesus said, 'Blessed are the pure in heart, for they will see God.' [Matthew 5:8] That purity of heart is not our own but comes from Christ alone!

"My hope is built on nothing less
Than Jesus' blood and righteousness…
Dressed in His righteousness alone,
Faultless to stand before the throne.
On Christ the solid Rock I stand;
All other ground is sinking sand."
(The Solid Rock, Edward Mote)

It is in Christ that we are able to praise God for his 'great salvation so rich and free!' (Cf., worship chorus by Seth and Bessie Sykes)

The acknowledgement of the perfection of the word of God made known to us in the Person of Jesus Christ, the Eternal Word, and the recognition that we cannot on our own live up to his standard, and the acceptance of divine grace in Christ are the foundation of faith. Jesus is just the right word to fit the rhyme and reason of our life with God. Indeed he is the alpha and omega -- the first and last letters of the Greek alphabet --

37

the beginning and the end. [Revelation 1:8] The Lord Jesus is the starting point, the <u>aleph</u>, for our life with God.

PROPHETS

ISAIAH - ON EAGLES' WINGS

But those who wait for the Lord shall renew their strength, they shall mount up with wings like eagles, they shall run and not be weary, they shall walk and not faint.
Isaiah 40:21-31

The title of today's message is not intended as an endorsement of the Philadelphia Eagles in today's Super Bowl! I searched Scripture for a verse that would give equal time to the Patriots, but didn't find one. However, the television news the other day brought to my attention a church sign in Massachusetts which noted that eagles appear 33 times in Scripture, while goat (Greatest Of All Time) appears 42 times, thus assuring the Patriots of victory by 9 points! Be that as it may, we turn this morning to the suggested Old Testament lesson that offers the imagery of God's people rising on the wings of eagles.

The eagle – the bird, not the ballplayer – is a majestic creature, fittingly tapped as the official symbol of the United States since 1782. It is beautiful in flight, powerful in stature, and ferocious in the hunt. I have seen eagles flaring above canyons and sweeping over lakes. This weekend is the annual festival of eagle watching at Reelfoot Lake in northwestern Tennessee, where some seventy raptors are known to visit. Today, though, we meditate on this text from Isaiah where the prophet declares that God's people will rise up on the wings of eagles.

A couple of years ago the beauty and power of this metaphor impressed me when I participated in the organizational service for a new church in Denver, and the special music for the occasion was the song "On Eagle's Wings" by Michael Crawford. The verses of the song recall the 91st Psalm, where the Lord is regarded as a fortress and refuge, sheltering the faithful under his wings, shielding them from the terror of the night and the flight of arrows by day. But the chorus, to my mind, picks up the sentiment from the fortieth chapter of Isaiah that is our focus today:

And He [God] will raise you up on eagle's wings,
Bear you on the breath of dawn,
Make you to shine like the sun,
And hold you in the palm of His Hand.

When you consider the historical context of this Bible passage, though, nothing could have been further from the minds of the people the prophet was addressing. Far from soaring with eagles, they were about as low as people can go. In 587 BC the Babylonian King Nebuchadrezzar had destroyed the city of Jerusalem at the end of a long and harsh campaign.

41

Jerusalem had been under siege for two years, resulting in terrible famine in the city. So the people who heard Isaiah's message had not only lost a devastating war, much as their northern kingdom neighbors had done over a century earlier, but they had been literally removed from their homeland and required to make the long trek to the conquering nation Babylon. Judah's king Zedekiah had been forced to watch his family put to death, then he was blinded and led away captive to spend the rest of his life in a Babylonian prison.

We can scarcely imagine what such an experience would be like. To be uprooted from your home, marched away as your city lies in smoking ruins, leaving behind the only nation and culture you have ever known, including the precious temple on Mount Zion that has been desecrated and burned, to have no idea what the future would hold in a foreign land where pagan idols dominated the spiritual scene and ruthless rulers had their way with citizens, to say nothing of deportees! No, we can't identify with this, fortunately. The closest the modern world may know of this are the refugee streams fleeing war-torn homelands, but even this tragic phenomenon represents a willful desire to leave, not the forced departure of the Babylonian exile.

It is not known for certain how many people were actually removed from Jerusalem and its environs over several deportations. The prophet Jeremiah, who had predicted his nation's doom, estimated the number to be 4,600 (Jeremiah 52:28-30), but that number could easily rise to 15,000 when women and children are included. So not all the residents of Judah were taken away, but those who remained behind were subject to privation and disease. The population of Judah at the time was an estimated 250,000, but by the time the first returnees from the exile came back to Jerusalem seventy years later, only about 20,000 people were left. The life of the exiles in Babylon was, in some ways, to be preferred over the experience of those who stayed in Palestine. They were, apparently, able to settle on farms or start businesses, and some even rose to positions of note. But we sense their sorrow in the opening lines of Psalm 137:

> "By the waters of Babylon, there we sat down and wept, when we remembered Zion. On the willows there we hung up our lyres. For there our captors required of us songs, and our tormentors, mirth, saying, 'Sing us one of the songs of Zion!' How shall we sing the Lord's song in a foreign land?"

It was to these exiles in Babylon that the prophet whom scholars refer to as Second (Deutero) Isaiah addressed his message from the Lord. His work is found in chapters 40 to 55 of our present Book of Isaiah. Even though he identified strongly with the pre-exilic prophets such as Jeremiah

42

who saw the downfall of the nation as divine judgment for the sins of the people, his Word from the Lord began in an entirely different key. "Comfort, comfort my people says your God." [40:1] The time of service has ended, the iniquity of the nation has been pardoned. Now, despite every appearance of degradation and loss, the Lord is restoring his people!

1. GOD IS SOVEREIGN

Nothing could have prepared the people of the exile for this amazing, good news! For them, all was lost. But here is this spokesperson for God -- one who has walked the trail of tears with them, one who eats the crumbs of shame with them, one who knows the terrifying uncertainty of life in exile – here this prophet of God declares that the Lord is even now rescuing his people. Just as at the time of the Exodus when Moses led the children of Israel out of Egypt, so Almighty God is bringing hope and new life to Israel.

The signs of this new life were just barely on the horizon, but they were there. Years had passed since the destruction of the holy temple, but the faith of the people had not failed. Since sacrifices could no longer be offered in worship on Mount Zion, a new way of worship developed based on the reading and proclamation of Scripture, prayer, and the singing of the Psalms. Bible scholars see the roots of synagogue worship in the exile.

The Second Isaiah, most especially, shed new theological light on the understanding of God's creation of the universe. Here in this passage, for instance, the prophet reminds the people that "the Lord is the everlasting God, the Creator of the ends of the earth." [40:28] In Babylon there was a supposedly powerful deity called Marduk. But from the prophet's standpoint, Marduk was lifeless, powerless in contrast to Yahweh, the living God of Israel. 'To whom will you liken God?' asks the prophet. 'A workman casts the idol in bronze and overlays it with gold, and then thinks it speaks and works wonders!' [40:18] Nowhere in the ancient world was there a concept of a national divinity allowing the defeat of his people in judgment, but that is precisely how the Lord Almighty worked. God, through his prophets, had repeatedly warned the nation of the coming devastation if they did not repent and turn to God, but the kings and leaders of the nation paid no heed. Now Isaiah proclaimed that the Lord is the sovereign God, and that what had been predicted now had come to pass.

Isaiah saw his role as a living reminder of who God is and what God has done. 'Have you not known? Have you not heard?' Yes, the people had known, they had been told the accounts of God's mighty acts in the history of the people, but they had forgotten. And in their sorrow for

43

the loss of their nation, they came to believe that God no longer heard their cry nor cared for their circumstances.

2. GOD KNOWS THE SUFFERING OF HIS PEOPLE

Isaiah heard the Lord say, 'Why do you people think your way is hidden from the Lord, that the Lord will ignore justice in your case?' [40:40:27] How easy it is for us to feel, when we experience something like an exile of the soul, that God is unaware of our situation. That fear may come in bereavement, or in family turmoil, or in illness. It may come in time of national crisis or personal tragedy. In such moments it is tempting to think that God could not bother himself with our little worries, to believe that God is aloof from the struggles of the world he has made. Not so, says that prophet of the exile. Not so, says our Savior Jesus Christ, too! The Lord Jesus noted that the Almighty sees every sparrow fall, knows the number of the hairs on our head! [Lk 7:7] If we human parents know how to give gifts to our children, how much more does God care for his children? [Mt 7:11]

God is not sleeping through the trials that plague us. [Ps 121:3-4] This passage from Isaiah affirms that God does not grow weary, nor does he lose strength in the myriad responsibilities that are God's alone. Instead, the Lord will empower the weak, strengthen the fainthearted, lift up the fallen. These are the words our Lord Jesus lived by! And they are our assurance today through him.

3. GOD SAVES THOSE WHO LOOK TO HIM

'They who wait for the Lord shall renew their strength, they shall mount up with wings like eagles, they shall run and not be weary, they shall walk and not faint." The exiles knew the feeling of running out of steam at the end of their long journey from home. They knew what it was to dread tomorrow, which in all likelihood would be worse than today. They understood the pain of being rootless and without hope. But just at that precise moment, when the judgment of God seemed overwhelming, the light of God's mercy began to shine.

So it is that the New Testament tells us that at just the right time, God sent his Son to die for the ungodly. [Rom 5:6] When it appeared all was lost, then the Savior came.

For some of us who suffer a fear of heights this idea of taking flight with eagles is not all that comforting! Yet clearly this language is intended to impress upon us the Lord's uplifting power to free those who have been enslaved by sin and circumstance, to release us from the bondage of self-loathing, or the mistreatment of others, or the addiction of egotism that withers our relationships. So it is that Scripture often looks to the heights,

44

to the heavens, as a way of speaking about the redemption and restoration God makes available to us.

There is a story from the Exodus that drives home this idea. In their wilderness wandering, suddenly the camp of Israel was infested with deadly serpents. The people cried out to Moses for relief, and Moses prayed to the Almighty. The Lord instructed him to erect a bronze serpent in the camp with the instructions that those who were bitten should look to the raised image for healing. [Numbers 21:9] It was this story, this image, that our Lord Jesus alluded to in his own ministry. 'Just as Moses lift up the serpent in the wilderness,' said Jesus, 'so must the Son of Man be lifted up. And if I be lifted up, I will draw all people to me.' [John 3:14]

Those who wait for the Lord, those who look to the Lord, will mount up on wings like eagles. We shall soar with our Savior!

JEREMIAH - ADVENT'S HOPE

In those days and at that time I will cause a righteous Branch to spring up for David; and he shall execute justice and righteousness in the land. Jeremiah 33:15

The first Sunday in Advent is sandwiched between Thanksgiving, Black Friday, and Cyber Monday, so it doesn't get much press except in the churches. But typically on this Sunday every year we light the first candle on an Advent Wreath, a candle often thought of as the Hope Candle because of references to the prophetic predictions of the Messiah.

Yet when we think of the Old Testament prophets, we don't ordinarily associate their message with hope. A warning, impending judgment, yes, a call to repentance certainly. But hope? Not so much. The season of Advent, though, leading to the Christmas celebration reminds us of prophetic promises to be fulfilled in the coming Messiah. Despite the dire pronouncements of the prophets, there is also in them an assurance of divine mercy and restoration, a message of hope.

1. ADVENT HOPE IN TOUGH TIMES

The prophet Jeremiah is a case in point. Sometimes referred to as 'the weeping prophet' because of the tenor of his oracles and his authorship of the Book of Lamentations, Jeremiah was no rose-colored glasses commentator. No Polly-Annish view of reality for him! On the contrary, he predicted, rightly, the downfall and exile of his nation, incurring the wrath of King Zedekiah. The Lord told him to put a yoke on his neck and show the king what the future holds for him! Another prophet named Hananiah took the yoke off Jeremiah and broke it, but he did so without the Lord's instruction. Soon Hananiah was no longer among the living! [Jeremiah 28:17] So upset was the king with one of Jeremiah's sermons that he cut up the parchment manuscript with his penknife! (Don't get any ideas!) The Lord did the king one better. He instructed his prophet to eat the next batch! Fortunately his amanuensis Baruch had made another copy. Jeremiah was taken into custody under heavy guard. In fact when the conquering Babylonians marched in, they offered Jeremiah a place of honor, which he refused. He wasn't on the side if the enemy. He was on the Lord's side.

So here was a man who saw the darkest days of his homeland, a man on the outs with the powers that be and his own neighbors, a man dissatisfied with the message God had given him. It would not be expected that Jeremiah would be a prophet of hope. But just when things got really bad and all chances of national survival were exhausted, the prophet had a visitor at the jail. His kinsman came to notify him that a parcel of land in

46

Anathoth was coming up for sale, and according to the custom of the day, Jeremiah had first right of refusal. What should he do? He's in prison, his city's besieged and going down, the nation seemed doomed. Why buy a piece of land with no assurance you'd have access to it in the future? The natural response would have been 'Thanks, but no thanks.'

Jeremiah, though, surprised everyone. He called his secretary Baruch to draw up the paperwork, weighed out the money on scales, signed the bill of sale before the correct number of witnesses, and sealed the document in a jar for safe keeping. Jeremiah believed in the future because Jeremiah believed in God! He had heard the Lord say to his people, 'I know the plans I have for you, plans for good and not evil, to give you a future and a hope.' [Jeremiah 29:11]

In today's reading the prophet proclaims: "Behold, the days are coming, declares the Lord, when I will fulfill the promise I made to the house of Israel and the house of Judah. In those days and at that time I will cause a righteous Branch to spring up for David, and he shall execute justice and righteousness in the land. In those days Judah will be saved, and Jerusalem will dwell securely. And this is the name by which it will be called: 'The Lord is our righteousness.'" [33:14-16] Looking at it from our vantage point, we realize the prophecy envisioned the coming of Jesus Christ. But the prophet only knew that God would be faithful to his promises, and in God's time, deliverance would come. The prophetic purchase of land, and the anticipation of a new leader were signs of the Advent Hope.

For us Advent is a time of reflective preparation for the Christmas celebration. Our Advent Hope is based on what we know of Christ and the salvation he has brought. But the prophets could see that only dimly as the Lord gave them vision. It is amazing how accurately they did predict his coming, though. The prophet Micah foretold that the Messiah would come from the little village of Bethlehem. [Micah 5:2] Hosea declared God's forgiveness and restoration despite the waywardness of the people. [Cf., Hosea 2:22-23] Habakkuk said something similar. The prophet Haggai urged the returning exiles to rebuild the temple, for it was to be a house of hope. [Haggai 2:9] And Malachi, the last of the Old Testament prophets, concluded with a prediction of the coming of Elijah and the age of the Messiah. [Malachi 4:5]

The Advent Hope arises not from times of prosperity, faithfulness and ease, but in times of stress, heartbreak and doubt. For Advent Hope is not like the world's hope. It doesn't come from a positive outlook. It isn't the product of a sunny disposition. It is based solely on the promise of our faithful God. During this time of pandemic we have revisited the theme of Biblical hope again and again. It is relatively easy to be hopeful when all is well. But it takes a special kind of faith to call on the Advent Hope when times are difficult.

2. ADVENT'S HOPE AND THE MESSIAH

Another thing to notice about the prophets' Advent Hope is the nature of the Messiah who was anticipated. Isaiah saw this more clearly than others. The coming Messiah was to be the Suffering Servant. [Isaiah 53] God's anointed would judge with righteousness and his rule would never end. But there would be nothing about him that would be like the rulers of the world. He would take in himself the wounds of the world. He himself would atone for our sins in his own flesh. Some of the Psalms envisioned this, too. [Cf., Psalm 22]

Needless to say, as the years went by the vision of a coming Messiah did not dwell on the suffering of God's anointed! More and more the expectation was for a political-military hero who would vanquish Israel's enemies and re-establish an earthly kingdom in the manner of David's golden age. But that wasn't the Advent Hope. It was something else — nationalistic ideals, wishful thinking in the face of oppressive foreign occupation, perhaps.

So when the Lord Jesus came, he went unrecognized by most. 'He came to his own but his own did not receive him.' [John 1:11] Nor did the message he shared engender much enthusiasm. 'If any would be my disciple, let him deny himself, take up his cross and follow me.' [Matthew 16:24] And again, 'one who saves his life will lose it and he who loses his life for my sake and the gospel will save it.' [Matthew 16:25] Yet what Jesus brought was the fulfillment of God's promise, the realization of genuine hope.

3. ADVENT'S HOPE IN THE NEW TESTAMENT

In the New Testament the Advent Hope is expressed as having come in Jesus Christ. First Timothy begins with the apostle's testimony that he is writing "by the command of God our Savior and of Christ Jesus our hope." [1 Timothy 1:1] 'According to God's great mercy,' writes Peter, 'he has caused us to be born again to a living hope through the resurrection of Jesus Christ.' [1 Peter 1:3] In Christ, says Paul, like Abraham of old we 'hope against hope,' and in the face of trial we take our stand on hope. [Romans 4:18] Christ in us, he tells the Colossians, is the hope of glory. [Colossians 1:27]

One of the most challenging affirmations about Advent's Hope in the New Testament is Paul's conviction that the hope we have in Christ does not disappoint. [Romans 5:5] We know what it is to 'get our hopes up,' only to suffer a letdown. We know what people mean when they speak of 'false hope,' that sometimes we can mislead ourselves, not wanting to

48

face a difficult truth. Then there is the desperation of 'hoping for the best,' when in fact we are steeling ourselves for the worst! But these are not the Advent Hope. For the hope we have in Christ will never disappoint us. God's promises are true, the new life he offers in Christ is real.

Our Christian hymns affirm this, too. Katharina von Shlegel wrote: "Be still my soul: thy God doth undertake to guide the future as he has the past. Thy hope, thy confidence, let nothing shake; all now mysterious shall be bright at last." Directly across the page in our hymnbook there is another less familiar hymn with the line: "In Thee alone, dear Lord, we own sweet hope and consolation." [J. Magdeburg] A more recent gospel hymn proclaims, "My hope is in the Lord, who gave himself for me, and paid the price of all my sin at Calvary." [N. Clayton] The hymn "The Solid Rock" refers to Jesus Christ as "all our hope and stay." [E. Mote] It begins with the affirmation, "My hope is built on nothing less than Jesus' blood and righteousness." And that brings us back to our passage from Jeremiah. The prophet foresaw a "righteous Branch," the coming Messiah, who would bring salvation to his people. Then they would be known by this name: 'The Lord is our righteousness.' In Christ, we are made new, reconciled to God, forgiven of sin, and granted an everlasting hope!

AMOS –SHEPHERD OF TEKOA

Then Amos answered Amaziah, 'I am no prophet, nor a prophet's son; but I am a herdsman, and a dresser of sycamore trees, and the Lord took me from following the flock, and the Lord said to me, 'Go, prophesy to my people Israel. Amos 7:14

Amos the prophet was an equal opportunity doomsayer! When he began his message at the shrine at Bethel, he cried: 'For three transgressions of Damascus, and for four, I will not revoke the punishment, says the Lord.' [1:3] He went on in that vein to tell of the judgment of Gaza, Tyre, the Ammonites and Moab. By this time he must have gathered quite an enthusiastic audience, because all these surrounding countries posed a threat to Israel. 'Yeah!' his listeners must have thought. 'Let 'em have it, Lord!' But then, as if drawing descending concentric circles on the geography of the region, Amos uttered an unexpectedly chilling indictment of Judah, Israel's near neighbor and sister nation to the south. 'For three transgressions of Judah and for four, I will not revoke the punishment, because they have rejected the law of the Lord. So I will send fire on Judah and devour the strongholds of Jerusalem.'

There might have been a few nervous gasps in the crowd when they heard this. It's one thing for the Lord to take vengeance on those idolatrous nations, but Judah? That was a little too close for comfort! Then they realized the prophet wasn't through. In a voice that could not be shouted down, he declared: 'Thus says the Lord, for three transgressions of Israel and for four, I will not revoke the punishment, because they sell the righteous for silver, and the needy for a pair of sandals.' [2:6] The pronouncement continued and the congregation became more agitated. 'I hate and despise your solemn assemblies, says the Lord. I will not accept your sacrifices.' [5:21-22] Amos said this right in the halls of those assemblies, right in front of the altar of sacrifice. Those gathered for worship heard this strange fellow from down south, who claimed to be speaking for God, say that God would not accept their worship! 'Take away from me the noise of your songs, says the Lord. But let justice roll down like waters, and righteousness like an ever-flowing stream!' [5:24]

1. A STANDOFF AT THE SHRINE

This sets the stage for one of the most memorable confrontations in Holy Scripture, the standoff between the shrine's priest Amaziah and the prophet Amos. As Amos' sermon became ever more frightening to the people, word got back to the rectory that there was a fellow in the sanctuary

50

causing trouble. Amaziah did not like to be interrupted from his priestly duties, but he decided to see for himself what the ruckus was about. Day after day in the shrine he presided over the prayers and sacrifices of the people. He felt the choir at Bethel measured up to anything Jerusalem had. Ever since the king had authorized this special sanctuary, Amaziah had considered it an honor to be in charge of the place. He wasn't about to have it disturbed by some rustic prophetic pretender. When he came through the doors of the sanctuary he heard that voice trumpeting.

'This is what the Lord showed me,' the man bellowed. 'He was forming locusts to destroy the land, but I prayed to God: I beg you, Lord, Israel can't take such a scourge. And the Lord relented, "It shall not be," he said.' At this Amaziah was fuming. The idea that this nobody was preaching in his shrine without permission galled him. But he bided his time and listened some more. Amos then said, 'Then the Lord showed me a shower of fire that would devour everything. But again I prayed for the people, and the Lord relented. "It shall not be," God said.' 'Ha!' thought Amaziah. 'This guy thinks he has that kind of influence with the Almighty! How absurd! But at least he says there will be no destruction from the Lord.'

Then in my mind's eye I see the prophet Amos looking up from the congregation to see the priest Amaziah standing smugly in the doorway. And the prophet speaks again: 'The Lord showed me a wall, and he had a plumb line in his hand. He said, What do you see, Amos? And I said, I see a plumb line. And the Lord said, I am setting a plumb line in the midst of my people Israel. And never again will I pass by.' [7:7-8] Never again. The Lord withheld the locusts and the fire, because of the prophet's intercession. But now the Lord's plumb line, God's standard of law and justice and righteousness, showed the true measure of Israel's waywardness. The prophet read out the verdict: 'The sanctuaries of Israel will be laid waste, and the house of King Jeroboam will be destroyed.'

When he heard that, Amaziah stormed out of the sanctuary and headed for the king's palace. He told Jeroboam what this would-be prophet had said, no doubt thinking the king would send soldiers to arrest him. But for some reason the king did not. So Amaziah hastened back to Bethel and confronted Amos himself.

2. A CLASH OF TITANS

It was a classic clash of spiritual titans. The iconoclastic prophet versus the self-satisfied priestly establishment. That sort of tension has always been there in the community of faith -- still is today. Usually the priestly caste and the government see more or less eye to eye. But the prophetic voice challenges the status quo, unimpressed by the trappings of grandeur in the holy places, not intimidated by the power of royal palaces. Amaziah sees his life's work undermined by this interloper. And he lashes out in ridicule and anger.

'O seer,' he says through clenched teeth, 'go back to Judah where you came from. Do your prophesying there for the two bits it's worth! Never again prophesy here at Bethel, the king's sanctuary.' But Amos stings Amaziah in return: 'I'm not a prophet, not even the son of a prophet. I'm a layperson from Tekoa, a farmer and herdsman. But the Lord took me from the flock and said, Go to Israel and prophesy. Here I am! And because you have prohibited me to speak, not only will this land be defeated and its people go into exile, but your own family will suffer a terrible fate.'

The book of Amos is part of the Twelve Minor Prophets in the Hebrew Bible. But there is nothing minor about Amos' message. He was the first of the classic eighth century (BC) prophets whose books bear their names. His ministry occurred during a time of almost unprecedented prestige and prosperity in the Northern Kingdom ruled by Jeroboam II. Neighboring lands had been conquered in battle, and the wealthy elite maintained a standard of living unknown before. But the inequities between the upper one percent and the remaining ninety-nine had grown immeasurably. The wealthy consolidated their holdings at the expense of the poor. Those in positions of power controlled the court system, saw to it that laws were enforced to the advantage of the rich, made it next to impossible for the little man to get justice. Family farms were lost to the greed of the powerful. All the while, Amaziah and those of his class took their places in the solemn assemblies at Bethel and elsewhere, singing hymns to the Lord in the expectation that God would bless them even more! It never occurred to them that their oppression of their own people would render their worship ineffective before God. Until Amos showed up, that is.

He might not have been a member of the prophet guilds that had become popular since the time of Elisha, but Amos was definitely a prophet! And far from being the backwoods rube Amaziah accused him of being, Amos was a person of some means, shepherding his own flocks, tending the fig trees of his property in Tekoa. He was no provincial Judean. He knew well the practices of the countries in the region. Perhaps he had commerce with them. For when the Lord opened his eyes to the problems in each of the nations, Amos reported it with pinpoint accuracy. That's what gave his comments about Judah and Israel so much punch. He was on target with the criticism of Judah, which claimed the inside track on the law of the Lord only to consistently bend it to their own will. And he was on the money with Israel (pardon the pun!), which had managed to use its prosperity to feed its greed.

52

3. THE MESSAGE TODAY

The message of the prophet needs a hearing today. There are sharp inconsistencies in our society, and the person of faith surely realizes that the Lord holds us all to account. We do hear complaints about injustice today, and often with good reason. What we hear much less of, though, is a concern about the lack of righteousness among us. Amos heard the Lord say: 'Let justice roll down like waters, and righteousness like an ever-flowing stream.' In other words, justice and righteousness go together. We cannot attain true justice without genuine righteousness. That is, a submission to the will and way of God is the foundation of justice among people! This is a missing piece in our understanding today.

There is another striking note in the message of Amos, too. After the bleak forecast of judgment, toward the end of his message, the prophet hears the Lord God say: 'On that day I will raise up the booth of David that is fallen, and repair its breaches and rebuild it as of days of old. I will plant them upon their land, and they shall never again be plucked up, says the Lord your God.' [9: 11, 15] In other words, out of the devastation of defeat and exile in punishment for sin, there is the hope of restoration and renewal in God! This is a theme that the prophets who came after Amos would take up as well. God's judgment of his people is intended to be redemptive, it is meant to offer new life in fulfillment of the divine covenant and in the people's faithfulness.

One more observation from this great book captures our attention. We saw that prophet and priest were at odds in the book. And the king, in wealthy expediency, was part of the problem. I noted that often there have been conflicts between the prophetic voices and the status quo priests and rulers. But there is an exception to this, and only one. His name is Jesus. A beloved gospel hymn by Fanny J. Crosby noted this. "Crown Him! Crown Him! Prophet and Priest and King!" Jesus alone is Prophet, Priest and King. In him alone is true righteousness in love, and justice with mercy. He is a champion of the poor, the downtrodden and dispossessed. He is a compassionate Ruler who gives himself for his people. Amos would have loved Jesus, had he been privileged to know him. In fact, the prophets – as represented by Elijah on the mount of Transfiguration – and the law, as represented by Moses – were shown to be under Christ's authority. John the Baptist, whose message and style remind us of a fellow like Amos, said it best: 'He who comes after me is before me. I am not worthy to tie his sandals. He must increase and I must decrease.' [John 1:27; 3:30] Amos would have felt the same way!

53

HABAKKUK – PROPHET OF FAITH

Look at the proud! Their spirit is not right in them, but the righteous shall live by their faith. But the earth will be filled with the knowledge of the glory of the Lord, as the waters cover the sea. But the Lord is in his holy temple; let all the earth keep silence before him. Habakkuk 2:4, 14, 20

Nineteen forty-seven was a banner year for biblical archeology. That was the year when a young Bedouin shepherd discovered several ancient earthen jars in a cave in the cliffs above the Dead Sea near a site known as Qumran. From that fortuitous moment, all the intrigue of a good mystery novel was set in motion, with scholars, church leaders and the state of Israel playing key roles. Ultimately teams of archeologists descended on the region and found some 900 fragments of biblical material that had been hidden in the Judean desert for two thousand years. Copies of parts of practically every book in the Hebrew Bible except Esther were found.

Many of the learnings from these priceless documents have filtered down into local churches through commentaries, Bible lessons, dissertations, sermons and the like. We know, for example, that there was a kind of Jewish monastic community in Qumran during the inter-testamental period for which the scrolls were like a community library. In addition to the biblical material they contained rules for the community and commentaries. This religious group, called the Essenes, may well have provided a home and spiritual grooming for the young John the Baptist. One of the jaw-dropping discoveries from the scrolls was a portion of the book of Habakkuk with a commentary, the earliest biblical manuscript discovered to date.

Habakkuk belongs to a series of Old Testament books called the Twelve Minor Prophets. The description "Minor Prophets" probably dates from the work of St. Augustine and has to do with the brevity of their books. I can relate to that category. It has not been my lot in ministry to serve in the vast cathedral, the packed sports stadium, the megachurch, or the television soundstage. Those high profile religious venues produce a celebrity type of ministry. Mine has been devoted to the more typical smaller church, the non-glitz variety. So it's encouraging to realize that our Bible has components that are comparatively small and not so well known. The New Testament has its minor sections, too. Think of the Letter of Jude, of Third John, and of Titus. Most of us would be hard pressed to come up with a single verse from any of those books. In contrast, though, the Twelve Minor Prophets of the Old Testament include some pretty famous names: Hosea and Amos, Jonah and Micah, for instance. But one of the least familiar of them is Habakkuk, just three chapters long.

In looking through my sermon files over many years of preaching, I could not find a single message from the book of Habakkuk. Today I want to correct that oversight. Actually, I have made reference to some of its memorable verses, texts that I will speak to today. Although I no longer have all my sermon notes, I think it's safe to say that I haven't spent as much time with Habakkuk as I have other parts of the Bible.

Part of the reason is that we don't know very much about this prophet. His name, Habakkuk, means something like a 'loving embrace,' and it's evident that the prophet had a deep love for his people and a love for God. His message is set between the fall of the northern kingdom of Israel at the hands of the Assyrians and the rise of the Babylonian Empire after the battle of Carchemish which established Nebuchadnezzar as a world leader. He would sack Jerusalem in 587 BC, destroy the Temple, and lead thousands into exile, ending the southern kingdom of Judah as an independent nation state. It was not until May 14, 1948, that a state of Israel would again take its place in world affairs. And of course, the Palestinian conflict has been regularly renewed ever since.

Unlike the prophet Amos, who was a shepherd and dresser of sycamore trees, we know nothing of Habakkuk's occupation. In distinction from Hosea, we have no inkling of his family life. We do not have the sense that he had the ear of the king in the way that Isaiah or Jeremiah did. His name is mentioned nowhere else in Scripture, though some of his comments find important echoes. But when he solemnly took his stand upon the watchtower in Jerusalem to keep an eye out for what the Lord was doing, listening for an answer to the question he posed, waiting for a word from God, Habakkuk became a spokesman of warning and of hope, a prophet of faith.

For not only did Habakkuk love his country and the Lord, he also had a concern for both. Habakkuk's message begins with a question addressed to the Lord, a complaint, really. 'How long, O Lord?' It's a question we ourselves are quite familiar with! We found ourselves asking it a year ago when the pandemic seemed to be getting on our last nerve after just a few months. Little did we know we'd still be dealing with some aspects of it halfway through 2021! The question, 'How long?' was raised by the Psalmist, too. 'How long will you hide your face from me, Lord? How long must I bear this pain? How long shall my enemy be exalted over me?' [Psalm 13:1-2] 'How long, O Lord, will you be angry forever?' [Psalm 79:5] Habakkuk wails, 'How long shall I cry for help and you will not listen? You who cannot even look on wrongdoing, why are you silent when the wicked swallow up the righteous?' Job raised the same kind of question. 'Why do the wicked live on, reach old age, and grow mighty in power? They spend their days in prosperity, saying to God, "Leave us alone!"' [Job 21:7, 13-14]

Jeremiah wondered, "Why does the way of the guilty prosper? Why do all who are treacherous thrive?" [Jeremiah 12:1] The Psalmist acknowledged the concern. 'I was envious of the arrogant, and saw the prosperity of the wicked. For they have no pain; they are not in trouble as others are.' [Psalm 73:3-5] At times we may wonder why the righteous Godly people suffer, though the wicked seem to have no problems at all? The issue is touched on by many Scripture passages. How is it fair that a righteous God who is in control of all things allows bad things to happen to good people, while the careless, indifferent wicked people seem to have no difficulties?

Habakkuk, a man of God, saw the perversion of justice, violence and wrongdoing on every hand. Those internal problems in his country were exacerbated by the growing threat of the Chaldeans, the people we know as the Babylonians, who were at the point of sending their ruthless army against Judah. But the prophet didn't see God doing much about any of it! I expect we, too, have had such concerns at times. The relaxation of moral standards in our day, the continuing struggle with violence, the systemic injustice, the political divisions, the international tensions – all of this makes us wonder why God hasn't done something about it! We can relate to Habakkuk. So he decided, figuratively speaking, to climb up the watchtower, to take his position on the city's ramparts, looking for the Lord. He was determined to listen for the Lord's answer to his complaint. And he was not disappointed.

But when the Lord answered, it contained a surprise. "Write the vision," said the Lord. 'Write it large enough on tablets so that even a runner could read it.' Habakkuk, like Jeremiah and other prophets, would write down the vision the Lord granted him. It was to be committed to paper, etched in stone, so to speak. There was to be no misunderstanding, no forgotten phrase. Thus a copy of the oracle of Habakkuk was found in a cave, preserved over two millennia in desert conditions. Yet the Lord did not directly answer the prophet's question. Instead, God sent a warning: 'Alas for you who heap up what is not your own! Alas for you who get evil gain! Alas for you who build a town by bloodshed, who make your neighbors drink from your wrath. For you will be sated with contempt instead of glory.' [2:6, 9, 12, 15, 16] Those who worship false gods, who fashion idols for themselves, will come to realize there is no breath in them. [2:19]

This is a response to the prophet's complaint. The desired divine action may be delayed, but it is surely coming! The Lord's answer offers no explanation as to the suffering of the innocent. But the answer itself is vindication of the prophet's question. In this second chapter of Habakkuk there are three wonderful verses that set Habakkuk apart as a prophet of faith. Here we find affirmation, acclamation and adoration.

1. AFFIRMATION

In the Lord's answer to the prophet's concern, we find a towering affirmation. Noting the haughtiness and arrogance of the wicked, the Lord says simply: "Their spirit is not right in them." Then this: "But the righteous live by their faith." [2:4b] If this has a familiar ring, it's because the apostle Paul used this verse as a kingpin of his own theology. He quotes this text twice, once in the Letter to the Galatians, and again in Romans. [Galatians 3:11; Romans 1:17] We know his statement as, "The just shall live by faith." The Letter to the Hebrews, encouraging readers to be steadfast in the face of trial, used this text from Habakkuk: 'my righteous one will live by faith.' [Hebrews 10:38]

The word translated faith in this verse can be rendered "faithfulness." The people of God will live by their faithfulness, by their steadfast trust in the loving, righteous Lord. Even though the days seemed dark to Habakkuk, yet he would trust in God. He realized, as the New Testament would later affirm, that we are not made righteous by our good deeds, not by our efforts to avoid sin, but only in our faith. For us, of course, that faith and faithfulness has been made possible through the atoning sacrifice of Jesus Christ our Savior. "Dressed in his righteousness alone, faultless to stand before the throne," says the old hymn. "On Christ the solid rock I stand, all other ground is sinking sand." [Edward Mote]

2. ACCLAMATION

Let me call your attention to another spectacular verse in this chapter. After the Lord pronounces his judgment on evil, we hear this resounding acclamation: "But the earth will be filled with the knowledge of the glory of the Lord, as the waters cover the sea." [2:14] That's the answer to Habakkuk's concern! The Lord would use the idolatrous and powerful nation Babylon to humble Israel for its sins, but Babylon would suffer a similar fate in time. And over it all, over all the intrigue and warring of the nations, over all the deceit and faithlessness of the people, the Lord's glory would fill all the earth as the waters cover the sea!

How true this is! Look at the world around us. "All nature sings and round me rings," says another hymn. [M.D. Babcock] Whatever may be happening in the news of the world – shootings, war, cyber-hacking and so much else – the grandeur of a mountain peak, the roar of an ocean wave against the shoreline, the flurry of a field of bluebonnets, the change of seasons all proclaim the glory of our Creator. And that is before we even mention those dearest relationships that warm our hearts and grant us a sense of belonging and purpose. Our time knows something of the darkness of evil and threat, but Habakkuk was living on the precipice of his nation's destruction. From the watchtower of his faith he saw the glory of the Lord filling all the earth!

3. ADORATION

The final verse of chapter two holds out the invitation for the adoration of the Lord. "But the Lord is in his holy temple; let all the earth keep silence before him." This verse reminds me that as a high school student I sang in our church choir, and this was one of our choral responses. Perhaps you have heard it somewhere along the line, too. This proclamation follows a passage in which the Lord God holds in derision worthless idols. The time in which Habakkuk served was packed with religions, but there was only one true faith in the Lord. Babylon had its gods, as had the other nations. But they were made by human hands, fashioned out of wood, stone and precious gems. And when their makers fell down to worship them, they heard nothing in reply. 'There is no breath in them,' said the Lord.

We may think a passage like this, with its attention to idols, betrays a primitive spiritual view that modern people would not countenance. But there are idols still, and most are not made of wood or stone, yet they are definitely of our own making! We can make the accumulation of goods and wealth an end in itself, an idol, if you will. We can champion our own personal rights and privileges to the extent that we become the center of the universe, an idol of our own making. We can support a political perspective, or a sports team, or a movie star to the point of fanaticism and idolatry. The perversity of idolatry is that it takes something that should be for our good and transforms it into something that is all consuming, and thus evil.

In contrast the Lord, the true and living God, is in his holy temple. And his temple, we know from the New Testament, is within us! "Do you not know," Paul asked the Corinthians, "that your body is a temple of the Holy Spirit, which you have from God, and you are not your own?" [1 Corinthians 6:19] The prophet Habakkuk recognized that despite the might of threatening nations with their callous deities, the Lord was still in charge, still in his holy temple. In awe, Habakkuk – and the rest of us – must bow in reverent silence.

HOSEA – TRANSFORMING LOVE

When the Lord began to speak through Hosea, the Lord said to him, "Go, marry a promiscuous woman and have children with her, for like an adulterous wife this land is guilty of unfaithfulness to the Lord."

"I will betroth you to me forever; I will betroth you in righteousness and justice, in love and compassion. I will betroth you in faithfulness, and you will acknowledge the Lord." Hosea 1:2; 2:19-20

One should exercise caution when speaking about the personal lives of biblical characters, I think. For one thing, often the information we have is sketchy, and it comes to us from a vastly different culture long ago, reflecting customs and norms that seem strange to modern readers. Yet in Scripture we find that unmistakable thread of common humanity, the realities of life and death, achievement and failure, joy and sorrow that we share with the people of the Bible. The world of the Bible is different, yet it still mirrors our own world and time, because it is the story of God's reaching out to the people created in God's own image. It is a story of hope and hurt, of judgment and redemption, of peace and conflict, of insight and misunderstanding. Despite the chasm of years that yawns between us and the flesh-and-blood folks of the Bible, we frequently can identify with them, suffer their heartache, rejoice in their triumph. Readily we see the mistakes they made, and there is the gnawing concern that perhaps we, under similar circumstances, would not do much better. We are grateful when this one or that turns to the Lord in faith and obedience, and we are scornful when others fail to do so. But we are restless in our own critique, because we realize we are not above reproach, either.

1. A SAD STORY

Today we turn to what must be acknowledged as one of the saddest stories in the Bible. It's not the only one, not even the saddest of all. For that we would have to look to the Garden of Eden, and then ultimately to the Garden of Gethsemane and the Cross of Calvary. There are plenty of other sad stories in Scripture, too. We think of Moses stepping off the mountain top experience of Mount Sinai with those tablets of stone in his arms, only to look down upon the camp of Israel and see the revelry around a golden calf! Or the treachery of Jacob and his mother when old Isaac was blind and on his deathbed. We might recall the murderous lust of King David who sent a valiant and loyal soldier to certain death because he

59

wanted the man's wife for his own. The tragic rift between two great Christian missionaries, Paul and Barnabas, the dark night of the soul for Peter in the High Priest's courtyard, the murder of John the Baptist – all sad stories. But the account of the prophet Hosea's marriage to a woman named Gomer must rank right up there with these others. We know that the Lord laid it on Hosea's heart to marry Gomer, but I can't help feeling that the story has the clarity of hindsight about it.

You may be familiar with this story, because the book of Hosea is more well known than some of the other Minor Prophets. It's longer than all but one of them, too. Zechariah alone equals the fourteen-chapter length of Hosea. Still, it is with a certain hesitancy that we peer into the highly personal account of Hosea's family situation. We bear in mind that we have only one side of the story – Hosea's. His wife Gomer has nothing to say in the book. Further, that she was characterized as being a promiscuous wife – a "wife of whoredom" in some translations [e.g. NRSV, RSV] – casts her in a very unfavorable light from the outset. Yet Hosea evidently loved her, because he went after her despite her having running off with others. So it is with some reluctance that we venture into the murky waters of this marital relationship. We do it at all only because the prophet insists on it, and he does so for one reason. His personal life is presented as a living parable –an object lesson, so to speak -- of the strained relationship between God and the people of Israel. The experience of Hosea and Gomer is the way the prophet speaks of Israel's infidelity to the Lord, and also of God's righteous indignation, and then finally God's mercy in restoring Israel to a covenant relationship that is as intimate and binding as marriage.

In reading the first chapter of this book we probably are most touched by the circumstances of the three innocent children born in this troubled family. To hear the prophet tell it, the Lord required him to marry this woman of sullied reputation, and then when she bore him children, the Lord instructed Hosea to give them specific, symbolic names. The first was named Jezreel, a word that means "God sows." But it was a place name in ancient Israel, the place where a bloody coup began the Jehu dynasty, of which the present King Jeroboam II was to be the last. The second child – a little girl – was to be named Lo-Ruhama, which meant "not pitied." It was a way of saying the Lord would no longer pity the people of Israel. Some translations have it "not loved." The third child was another son called Lo-Ammi, meaning "not my people." The Lord told Hosea that this was to show that Israel was no longer God's people, nor was God their God! Bible names often had symbolic significance, we know, but these seem a bridge too far for us. There is some indication in the text that Hosea questioned whether or not he was the father of these last two. But regardless, perhaps you'll agree that the people we feel sorriest for in the story are these

60

innocent kids! Let's hope Hosea had pet names for these youngsters. In my imagination I think of little Jezzy playing in the backyard, and his younger sister Loma with a favorite doll, and tiny Lammy in diapers bouncing on his Dad's knee. Maybe that's not so far-fetched after all, because toward the end of chapter two the Lord adds further comment to these names. Of the Valley of Jezreel God says he will cause the earth to respond with grain and new wine and olive oil. Prosperity, in other words, a time of peace and plenty. Then as for the little girl named "Not Loved," the Lord says, "I will show my love to the one I called 'Not my loved one.'" And of Lammy, "not my people," God says, 'You really are my people, and you know that I am your God!' [2:22-23]

2. LOOK FOR GOMER

The third chapter of the book is the shortest, just five verses long, only three paragraphs. In it Hosea is told by the Lord to go looking for Gomer, though she is with another man, and try to win her back. "Love her as the Lord loves the Israelites," he's told. So Hosea finds her and has to pay her pimp fifteen shekels of silver and about 450 pounds of barley worth another fifteen shekels. Thirty pieces of silver. Sound familiar? [Matthew 26:15] According to Exodus it was the typical price to buy a slave's freedom, or to compensate an owner whose slave was killed. (Exodus 21:32) It was called redemption.

There are many levels of heartache in this story. We could note parenthetically that one modern reference point could be the blight of human trafficking that enslaves over forty million people worldwide for purposes of sex trade and forced labor. Gomer, apparently, consented to her life of promiscuity, but these do not. Another relevant observation from the story is that in Hosea's time, Baalism was a continuous threat to the worship of the Lord. In essence that was a fertility cult, and one of its features was temple prostitution. It is intriguing that in English the words adultery and idolatry sound similar. For Hosea and the other prophets of the period, idolatry was the cardinal sin of the people of Israel, and it was often symbolized by adultery, the infidelity of the people toward God. If you were to rate the sin of idolatry on a scale of one to ten in our day, how high would you rate it? Probably not very high. But there are idols today, not simply images of precious metals and jewels, but other values in modern society that vie for first place in our lives.

So Gomer – she's not named in this chapter – returns with Hosea, though he makes it clear that they are not to engage in normal marital relations for a time. This is to signify the fact that the Israelites will be "many days without king or prince," and that they will not be able to offer sacrifices in the stone temple, presumably because it will be destroyed. But afterward, says the prophet, the people will return to the Lord their God and there will be blessings in the last days.

3. REDEMPTION AND RESTORATION

It's a sad story, yes, until we get to chapter three where we hear of redemption and restoration. The story of Hosea and Gomer's initially ill-fated marriage is a sad story, but it's not the whole story. Although the book of Hosea continues for another eleven chapters, nothing more is said specifically about that marriage. Based on the historical information we can deduce from the book, Hosea's ministry spanned almost fifty years. You would have thought that somewhere during that time he might have referenced specifically those first rocky years, or that he might have brought the reader up to speed on what really happened in the family. Instead, the prophecy continues, alluding to Israel's unfaithfulness which again is termed idolatry as well as adultery. The remainder of the book sees a seesaw of emotions. For instance there's the seemingly genuine repentance of the people in chapter six, which begins: 'Come, let us return to the Lord; for it is he who has torn, and he will heal us.'[6:1] But by chapter eight we hear the Lord say that Israel has 'sown the wind and will reap the whirlwind.' [8:1] 'Their heart is false,' says the Lord, 'and they must bear the guilt.' [10:2] But in chapter eleven God declares, 'When Israel was a child I loved him, and out of Egypt have I called my son.' [11:8] That verse, of course, was remembered when Joseph and Mary took the infant Jesus into Egypt. [Matthew 2:15] And so we hear the Lord say, 'How can I give you up, O Ephraim? I am the Lord your God, and besides me there is no Savior.' [12:4]

It has been said that the book of Hosea is a heart-felt message from a heart-sick prophet about a heart-broken God. [Skip Heitzig] That is certainly true, as far as it goes. But it doesn't go quite far enough! There is more to this story.

To get to that, let me recount an experience I had many years ago working as a counselor in a summer camp. The leader was a minister friend of mine, and his wife was with him for the week. He was doing an admirable job managing a couple hundred teens and the adult staff. But nearly every day he would do or say something that his wife, who was serving on the staff, felt obliged to criticize or ridicule. Maybe it was a tough time for them. It happens. But my friend never lost his cool with her, usually just chuckling as if to say she was right, after all. Twenty years later I was invited to share in another conference and was told the two of them would be there. I was hesitant about accepting the invitation. But in the end I did go. And wonder of wonders, their relationship was completely different! She was so supportive of him, and he so tender toward her! As I reflected on this later it came to me that love transformed the difficult to the precious. His love for her, her love for him, God's love for them both! Transforming love.

I believe that's what Hosea is pointing toward: the transforming love of God. I don't know if Gomer and Hosea were truly reconciled, but I believe they were. God was in that. And the sad story has an unexpectedly joyous ending. Sort of like the way that first Good Friday gave way to Easter. It's the story of the redemptive, transforming love of God who will not let us go, even when we are faithless, idolatrous, self-centered and self-deceived. God loves us with an everlasting love. It changes us. It redeems us. It brings us home.

The story of Hosea and Gomer reminds us, too, that in the New Testament we notice the followers of Christ are mentioned as the bride of Christ. (John 3:29; Revelation 21:2) The annals of church history reveal that the cycle of rebellion, repentance and restoration observed in the Old Testament is evident also in the life of the church. There have been times of lethargy and waywardness in the Christian community, as well as times of renewal and faithfulness. Yet the transforming love of God revealed in the perfect sacrifice of our Savior will one day present the bride of Christ without blemish in his eternal Kingdom.

There is a hymn that is especially fitting as we consider God's transforming love. Let me share a couple of its verses with you.

> O Love that wilt not let me go, I rest my weary soul in thee;
> I give thee back the life I owe, that in thine oceans depths its flow
> May richer, fuller be.
>
> O Joy that seekest me through pain, I cannot close my heart to
> thee; I trace the rainbow through the rain, and feel the promise is
> not vain, That morn shall tearless be. [George Matheson]

JOEL - AUTUMN RAIN

Be glad, people of Zion, rejoice in the Lord your God, for he has given you the autumn rains because he is faithful. Joel 2:23-32

What some call coincidence, I often call Providence. It's when two or more seemingly unrelated matters converge to produce sometimes a beneficial surprise. This happened to me this past Monday. It was a day that began with storm warnings and sirens, high winds producing what eventually would be termed an EF1 tornado a few miles from our home. Unfortunately, there were several homes damaged due to falling trees and limbs, and thousands of households were without power for days. But in the aftermath of that ragged beginning, there followed a refreshing autumn rain that lasted almost all day.

Later that morning I reviewed the suggested Bible readings for this Sunday. The Gospel reading was the famous parable of the Pharisee and tax collector, but I remembered that I've used that text here in the not so distant past. I turned then to the Epistle reading, and it was from Second Timothy, a continuation of last Sunday's lesson, and I was concerned about being too repetitious. I finally got around to looking up the proposed Old Testament reading, of which there were two. I took the first one and that's as far as I got. Because in the reading from the Book of Joel there was a reference to -- autumn rain! It just so happened that I was reading from the NIV, though most often I use the NRSV. Had I been reading the Revised Version, I wouldn't have noticed the coincidence, because the translation there is "early rain," rather than "autumn rain."

In the arid Bible lands, there are two seasons when farmers expect rain. The early rain, or autumn rain, comes in our months of October-November, just before the planting for a new season. The later rain, or spring rain, occurs close to harvest time in our months of April and May. Call it coincidence or Providence, I felt led to study the passage more closely, and the result is our meditation this morning.

If some of this reading from the Old Testament sounded familiar to you, it's probably because we hear it referred to at least every Pentecost Sunday. The apostle Peter quoted from the Book of Joel when he preached the first Christian sermon on that day. "In the last days, God says, I will pour out my Spirit on all people." [Acts 2:17] This verse, for Peter, explained the amazing manifestations of the Holy Spirit on Pentecost. And it became the groundwork for his proclamation of Jesus of Nazareth as the Messiah of God, who, though cruelly put to death, God raised from the dead. Peter and the rest of the apostles were witnesses of these events, and they were also recipients of the promised Holy Spirit because the risen

64

Christ poured it out on them! From that day, the apostles lived, spoke, acted and died in the power of the Spirit. It had been foretold by the prophet Joel.

Practically nothing is known about Joel, except that he was the son of a man named Pethuel (or Bethuel, take your pick). His name, Yoel, means "Yahweh is God," surely a truth emphasized again and again in the prophetic writings. The fact that he shows familiarity with Jerusalem and its environs leads to the notion that he lived there, and his interest in the faithful resumption of Temple worship suggests he may have been from the priestly caste. Even the date of the Book has scholars scratching their heads. In distinction from other prophets, he does not mention the name of the current king. This fact in itself has fostered the notion that perhaps Joel's ministry occurred in that in-between time when, following the death of Judah's only ruling Queen Athaliah (842-836 BC), her son (Joash) became king. But he was too young to rule, so the high priest actually became the go-to guy until the boy came of age. In effect, this was a time when there was no king! If that were Joel's time frame, he would have been a contemporary of the prophet Elisha. Other scholars disagree, noting that references in the Book seem to infer a post-exilic period, a time after the return of the people from Babylon some three hundred years later! The main historical reference point in the Book is the infestation of a horde of locusts, which is the occasion for the writing. But that was not an uncommon experience and cannot therefore be used to date it.

When you read the Book of Joel – by the way, you can do that in one sitting, it's only three chapters long! – you'll notice that while the prophet calls on the people to return to God, there is no specific mention of sins they have committed! Unlike Amos and Hosea, Jeremiah and the rest, Joel does not identify the sins of idolatry, or the abuse of the poor, or immorality, or injustice, or sketchy national alliances. The Book is a clear call to return to God in response to the agricultural crisis brought on by the plague of locusts, which Joel understood to be evidence of divine judgment. In Scripture, as distinct from popular culture, God's judgment is actually a necessary and beneficial, if terrible, thing! [Erin Dufault-Hunter, Ekklesia Project] But the reasons for the people's estrangement remain subject to speculation. Joel offers no scathing critique of Israel's behavior, just an urgent plea that the people should return to the Lord. This may be one of the ways the Book can be helpful to us! Since it does not specify the wrongdoing, we may find ourselves, and our own shortcomings, addressed. And that's a good thing, because otherwise this jaunt down ancient history lane wouldn't mean much!

There is in Joel's prophecy a three-pronged characterization of humanity's relationship to God that is in fact observed often in Scripture.

65

1. REALIZATION

First, there has to be some level of awareness of our desperate spiritual condition. On our own, though, we rarely come to this awareness. Everybody in Judah was suffering from the tragic effects of the devastating plague of locusts that left the fields bare. This caused hunger and want throughout the region. And along with the insects there was a severe drought. But only one person saw this natural disaster as in any way related to the spiritual health of the people. He was Joel, the prophet of God. To Joel came the realization that these severe living conditions were a sign of God's call to the people to turn away from their spiritual complacency and reconnect with the God of their forbears.

The other day I saw a bit of an interview with the Olympic swimmer Ryan Lochte. Though he is a twelve-time Olympic medalist, what he is most remembered for are his unfortunate more or less public displays of poor judgment, especially in the aftermath of the Rio Olympics. In the interview he was asked pointedly when he first realized that alcohol was a big part of the problem. He answered, "Only about a year ago." The rest of the nation knew there must be a problem of this kind long before, but it took a while for Ryan to realize it. To me, this is a reminder of human nature itself. Even when we know something's wrong, we tend to want to ignore that. We are resistant to the input of others, because of course we know what's best for ourselves!

If you had asked ordinary folks on the street in Jerusalem why the locusts had descended on the region, and why the wells were drying up, they would have simply shrugged and said, "Don't know. Happens every so often." They would not have seen in this experience any reason for spiritual concern. It would not have dawned on them that God was trying to tell them something. But Joel, the prophet of God, knew.

It makes us wonder, then, if there might be some signs around us in our own day that we could be missing. In general our lives are pretty good. But there are some unsettling things going on around us – natural disasters like earthquakes, devastating hurricanes and tornados, raging wildfires, terrifying infectious diseases. Not to mention the man-made calamities of mass shootings, terrorism, abuse of power, and so on. Does the person of faith begin to ask if there is something wrong spiritually?

Truthfully, we cannot come to a genuine relationship with God until we realize we need one! It may take the word of a person like Joel to help us see that need.

2. REPENTANCE

Joel was not content simply to point out the problem. There are many people today who are quick to point to what's wrong with the nation, or the community, or the church! But it's another matter to offer solutions. In the case of our Bible passage, the prophet urged the people to repent. Actually, he was more specific than that. He challenged the elders and the priests of the Temple to don sackcloth and call a solemn assembly of the people in the house of the Lord. They were to mourn their spiritual condition with fasting and cry out to the Lord. He didn't issue just a wholesale call to repentance, but he started with the spiritual leaders of the nation! Evidently Joel considered that they were responsible for the lackadaisical attitudes of the populace, and it would be up to them to call the people back to God. But first they must themselves repent!

In our own day the need for repentance may not be as obvious. We have become inured to the presence of sin and faithlessness for so long that we are surprised, and even a little chagrined at the suggestion that we, or our spiritual leaders, should repent and return to God! We wonder how we might react if we saw the community's spiritual leaders gather in one of the churches just for the purpose of confessing sin to God! How unseemly, we might think.

Genuine repentance doesn't come naturally to us. On the contrary, we are of the mind that there is precious little for which we might need to repent! Perhaps we are willing to concede that others, even ministers and priests and the church hierarchy, have good reason to repent, but the rest of us, not so much. But when the apostle Peter was asked on that first Pentecost Sunday, 'What must we do?' he answered, 'Repent, and be baptized in the name of Jesus Christ!' [Acts 2:38] Just as Jesus began his earthly ministry by calling the people to repentance because the kingdom of God was at hand, so the early church recognized that genuine faith can arise only from a realization of our need of a Savior, and in repentance of our sins. Unfortunately, the prophet's call to repentance often falls on deaf ears in our own time, as it did in the time of Joel.

3. RESTORATION

There is also in the Book of Joel a phrase that will run straight through the other prophets and into the New Testament. It is the "Day of the Lord." Clearly this concept depicts a time of reckoning, when God Almighty will judge the sins of the people. It's not necessary for us to go into detail about contemporary sins, any more than it was necessary in Joel's day. We could notice the societal slide toward a disregard for divine Law, the systemic subjugation of certain races and classes of people, the woes of

67

suppression of human rights and dignity, genocide and warfare, rampant crime, and much more. Few serious people of faith could doubt that the times in which we live manifest signs of spiritual sickness.

Yet the Day of the Lord for the prophet of Joel also meant a promise of divine restoration when and if the people truly turn back to God. The locusts will fly somewhere else, and there will be refreshing autumn rains that will replenish the wells that have gone dry, and cause the crops to grow once more, so that people and animals can be fed! Then the prophecy for which the little Book is most famous is uttered. "I will pour out my Spirit on all people," says the Lord. "Your sons and daughters will prophesy; your old men will dream dreams and your young men will see visions. Even on my servants, both men and women, I will pour out my Spirit in those days." [Joel 2:28-29]

Peter was so right to appropriate these verses for the first Christian sermon! This is a clarion call to the gospel of Jesus Christ. For the call of God is not a call to strict regulations that stultify the spirit as so many in our day seem to think. It is a call to life abundantly! It is an awakening to the Spirit of God that transforms society and does away with discrimination and prejudice, establishing the law of love in Christ and enabling the message of reconciliation to take root in relationships that have seemed most estranged. St. Paul would affirm it many years after Joel: 'In Christ there is neither Jew nor Gentile, male nor female, slave nor free, for all are one in Christ Jesus.' [Gal 3:28] The gospel is the great dignifier of humankind! It restores peace with God and neighbor and ushers in the age of the divine Kingdom of righteousness, integrity and wholeness in Christ.

MICAH OF MORESHETH

He has showed you, O man, what is good; and what does the Lord require of you but to do justice, and to love kindness, and to walk humbly with your God? Micah 6:8

We turn today, as we continue our review of some of the Minor Prophets from the Hebrew Bible, to the work of the last of the great eighth century BC prophets, Micah. His name, a shortened version of Micaiah, means "Who is like Yahweh?" And it's interesting that the final chapter of the book contains that very question. "Who is a God like you, pardoning iniquity and passing over the transgression of the remnant of your possession?" [7:18 NRSV] It's one of several memorable texts in this little book. It's in Micah that we hear the famous prediction that "they shall beat their swords into plowshares, and their spears into pruning hooks; nation shall not lift up sword against nation, neither shall they learn war anymore." [4:3] Micah declares, "As for me, I will look to the Lord, I will wait for the God of my salvation; my God will hear me." [7:7] And practically every Advent we share a verse from Micah that says, "But you, O Bethlehem Ephrathah, who are little among the clans of Judah, from you shall come forth for me one who is to be ruler in Israel, whose origin is from of old, from ancient days." [5:2] That verse finds its fulfillment, of course, in the nativity stories of our Lord Jesus in the Gospels of Matthew and Luke. Yet no text in the Old Testament surpasses the spiritual and ethical teaching of the one selected as the basis for today's message. In it the prophet affirms that the Lord has shown humankind what is the ultimate good in life, and what God requires of people: to do justice, love kindness and walk humbly with God. [6:8]

Let me hasten to say, however, that the book of Micah is not all sweetness and light! His pronouncements of divine judgment against Samaria in the Northern Kingdom and Jerusalem in the south are spine tingling. From the prophet's standpoint, the sins of Israel have been contagious, infecting the land of Judah. [1:9] The wickedness he sees includes the oppressive practices of large landowners, the unjust decisions of bribed rulers and judges, the infidelity and profiteering of priests and official prophets who proclaim "peace" in the face of idolatry and superficial worship. 'In that day, says the Lord, I will cut off sorceries and images, and you shall bow down no more to the work of your hands, and in anger and wrath I will execute judgments.' [5:12-13, 15] So, like some of the other prophets we have studied, there is a juxtaposition of righteous judgment followed by surprising mercy and restoration. This sequence happens three times in the book.

Micah was from the village of Moresheth situated about twenty-five miles southwest of Jerusalem in the foothills between the coastal plains and the central highland region of Palestine. Today the place is known as Marissa, an Arabized form of Moresheth. We're told that the village today is not much changed from the time of Micah. In his day it was a border town, precariously positioned between Judah and the country of the Philistines. As such it was continually susceptible to attack by forces interested in making war against Judah, forces such as the Assyrian army that tried twice to conquer Judah after having defeated Israel in the north, first in 711 and again in 701 BC. But in both instances the enemy forces were repelled, and this gave credence to the popular teaching that Jerusalem and its Temple could not possibly be overrun, because the glory of the Lord dwelt there. Micah was having none of it! Samaria had gone down, and so would Jerusalem in due time. But in fact the Southern Kingdom did not succumb for a long time. For this reason, Micah's prophecy lost some of its credibility. But it was revived when the prophet Jeremiah, a hundred years later, quoted Micah. He said, "Micah of Moresheth, who prophesied during the days of King Hezekiah of Judah, said to all the people of Judah: 'Thus says the Lord of hosts, Zion shall be plowed as a field; Jerusalem shall become a heap of ruins." [Jeremiah 26:18] Jeremiah, facing the onslaught of the Babylonians, knew the sad truth of what Micah had predicted a century before.

Micah stood in the line of some great prophets. There was a fellow named Eliezer who was from the same small town two hundred years before Micah. He prophesied against King Jehosophat of Judah because of his alliance with the wicked King Ahaziah of Israel. Micah, whose message of concern for the poor reminds us so much of Amos, must have been influenced by that profound shepherd of Tekoah because Amos's home was only twenty miles from Marosheth, and Micah was just a few years younger than Amos. Likewise, Micah was a younger contemporary of the first Isaiah, and of Hosea. These four prophets produced the golden age of Hebrew prophecy in the latter half of the eighth century BC. But while Isaiah was of aristocratic background in the capital city of Jerusalem, and Hosea was a prosperous farmer in the northern Kingdom, and Amos was a man of some means who prophesied in the shrine at Shiloh, Micah was an artisan, a country prophet. Apparently he delivered his message on various trips to the Holy City. And evidently his dire warnings had a sobering effect on King Hezekiah, who instituted some religious reforms in the wake of Micah's preaching. But all too soon the old ruinous practices returned and Judah ultimately suffered destruction and exile as had Israel years before.

Now I invite you to explore with me one of the great mountain peaks of Old Testament faith, this verse from Micah chapter six: *"He has showed you, O man, what is good; and what does the Lord require of you but to do justice, and to love kindness, and to walk humbly with your God?"* There are other peaks in this magnificent mountain range, too. Consider Deuteronomy 6:4-5: "Hear, O Israel: the Lord is our God, the Lord alone. You shall love the Lord your God with all your heart, and with all your soul, and with all your might." This would be followed closely by Leviticus 19:18b: "But you shall love your neighbor as yourself." Amos reveals another great height: "Let justice roll down like waters, and righteousness as an everflowing stream" [5:24] And in the book of Jonah just a few pages before Micah's words we hear the prophet complain, "I knew you were a gracious God and merciful, slow to anger, and abounding in steadfast love, and ready to relent from punishing." [4:2] Today, though, we take our place in a courtroom gallery the prophet has drawn where the Lord God has brought a case against Israel and asks the accused to speak.

1. WHAT THE LORD REQUIRES

Israel takes the stand and the court falls silent. 'With what shall I come before the Lord?' the witness asks. 'Shall I bring burnt offerings, yearling calves? Even thousands of rams, ten thousand rivers of oil would not be enough. Giving my firstborn for my sins, would that work?' Israel slumps in the chair, knowing there is nothing he can offer to cover his sinfulness.

Then the prosecutor speaks. 'The Lord has showed you, O man, what is good; and what is it the Lord requires of you?'

What has the Lord showed his people? Micah has already reminded his hearers of God's mighty rescue when they were enslaved in Egypt. 'I brought you up from the land of Egypt, and redeemed you from the house of slavery,' says the Lord. [6:4] There were other saving acts in the sacred history of these people, including the giving of the law through Moses, and the sending of judges and prophets to guide them, the possession of the Promised Land. Once they had been awed by those spiritual mountain peaks. But now the people had fallen into a spiritual amnesia. They had forgotten what God had done, and because of this they no longer could recall exactly what God requires of humanity. So they busied themselves with religious-feeling acts of sacrifice and worship. And if it made them think they were doing well to sacrifice to one God, perhaps it would make them feel even better to offer sacrifices to a few other deities, too! So the genuine religious service to the Lord had been diluted and corrupted. All the while, the nation was sinking lower and lower into the abyss of sinful, unethical, immoral behavior, thinking their Temple worship would absolve them of any wrongdoing. But the Lord, through Micah, called them into court. 'What does the Lord require of you?'

71

It's the question that still writes itself across the tablet of the thinking person's mind and heart. If we are God's creation, human beings created in God's own image, what is expected of us, what are we to do, how are we to live? There are many answers to the question. But in our passage today the Lord gives the superlative response.

2. JUSTICE, KINDNESS, HUMILITY

God has told you what is good and has showed you what is required: to do justice, to love kindness and to walk humbly with your God. Someone will say, "Oh, is that all?' But a moment's reflection will show how profound and challenging this is. To do justice means to act with fairness and honesty at all times and with all people. It means to champion the cause of those who are mistreated, to be on the lookout for injustice in society and in our own attitudes. We really have no idea of what true justice is apart from the will of God as revealed in his Word. And the quest for justice is a continual struggle in the courts and legislatures of the world. It is not easily attained, and it is readily compromised. Intentional deception and disinformation in politics, business, the media, religion or any other endeavor is an egregious injustice with catastrophic results. The substitution of revenge for justice, erroneously citing an eye for an eye, leaves everyone half-blind. For the fullness of divine justice, we must look to the gospel enfleshed in Jesus Christ.

This business of loving kindness, what is that about? The Hebrew word translated "kindness" can also be rendered "mercy." It is '*hesed*,' and it has to do with loyalty to the covenant the Lord has made with God's people. Because we have received mercy, we are to be merciful people. Having experienced unmerited grace, we are to delight in granting others something like that when it is within our capacity to do so. To live in the mode of kindness is not something that comes naturally to us. But this is what the prophet heard the Lord say as a divine expectation of his people. Once again, our concept of kindness and mercy is incomplete without the example and teaching of the Lord Jesus.

The third aspect of what the Lord requires is to walk humbly with our God. In an age that puts a premium on tooting our own horn, the me-first generation has some challenges when it comes to humility. And humility with God, at that! It is to recognize that we are not our own, that we have been created for God's purposes, and that we are fully accountable to God for what we do and say. Israel and Judah had lost sight of that somewhere along the line. And that forgetfulness can affect us, too. To walk humbly with God is to be submissive to God's will and not our own. Thus we remember our Lord saying, "Not my will but yours be done." So

72

this quiet little verse from the prophet Micah packs plenty of challenge for any of us.

3. FAITH AND WORKS

In Micah's time the primary problem he saw among his countrymen was a superficial, lifeless faith. It didn't effectively shape people's lives. They made their decisions without reference to God's will. And so the prophet called them to make their much-vaunted faith evident in what they were actually doing, how they were really living. 'Never mind the rituals of the Temple, just show me your faith by what you do,' he seemed to say! How very much like the book of James in our New Testament this is. We know that we are saved by grace through faith. [Ephesians 2:8] But we also recognize that the natural outgrowth of faith is righteous living. For as James put it so forthrightly, 'faith without works is dead.' [James 2:17]

This passage from Micah is a high point in Old Testament faith, but it is not the highest or greatest peak in the Biblical mountain range. We can understand and apply it most fully when it is read in the light of the gospel. For the Lord Jesus embodied the perfection of divine justice, mercy, kindness, meekness and submission to the will of the heavenly Father. Through him we – who can never expect to live up to the justice, kindness and humility Micah called for – through him we find hope and grace.

OBADIAH - REALLY?

For the day of the Lord is near against all the nations. As you have done, it shall be done to you; your deeds shall return on your own head... But on Mount Zion there shall be those that escape, and it shall be holy... Those who have been saved shall go up to Mount Zion to rule Mount Esau; and the kingdom shall be the Lord's.
Obadiah 15, 17, 21

Several years ago I asked a class of seminary students I was teaching as an adjunct faculty member what their favorite book of the Bible was. It was a group of about thirty adults, both men and women, representing a cross-section of ethnicities. As I anticipated, a number of them mentioned John, Matthew or another of the Gospels, though second in the unscientific poll was the book of Psalms. Some referred to the Letters of Paul. What I wasn't prepared for was the response of one of the young men who declared that his favorite was the Old Testament book of Obadiah. Obadiah, really? Intrigued, I asked him what made this rather obscure little book his choice. "It's because my middle name is Obadiah," he laughed. Whether he ever actually read the book of Obadiah or not I don't know, though I expect he did. But his name seemed as good a reason as any for his preference.

This summer I've felt challenged to devote a few sermons to some of the lesser known portions of Scripture. A couple of weeks ago we focused on the book of Habakkuk, and today we turn to another of the Twelve Minor Prophets, the book of Obadiah. The prophet's name means "servant of Yahweh," but other distinguishing features of the man are not to be found. Nothing of his personal biography is known. His book has the distinction of being the shortest one in the Hebrew Bible. Just one chapter in length, it still is not quite as brief as Third John in the New Testament that has just fifteen verses. But with its twenty-one verses, Obadiah is a tad shorter than Jude or Philemon which have only twenty-five verses each. Despite its brevity, this Old Testament book is specifically mentioned by the prophet Joel who, like Obadiah, foretells the coming day of the Lord. [Cf., Joel 2:2] There are some echoes of Obadiah in the work of Jeremiah, too, or perhaps it is vice versa. Because the historical setting for this book seems to have been sometime after the fall of Jerusalem to the Babylonians, and perhaps even after the return of the exiles. So Obadiah's ministry evidently took place before Joel's, but maybe sometime after Jeremiah's. Beyond that, it's tough to pinpoint the date of the book. The prophet's message is basically a divine indictment against the neighboring nation of Edom.

Tradition had it that the Edomites were descendants of Esau while the Judeans were descendants of Jacob, a story we know well from the book of Genesis. [Cf., Genesis 25:27-34] And the sibling rivalry and animosity between those brothers of antiquity is quite evident still in the work of Obadiah. The Lord's anger has been kindled against Edom, said the prophet, because they had treated their neighbor Israel so poorly. For instance, during the Exodus when the children of Israel were approaching the Promised Land, the land of Edom would not allow them to cross their territory. But nearer to Obadiah's time the problem was, when the Babylonian army was arrayed against Jerusalem, their Edomite neighbors to the south did nothing to help. In fact, when refugees sought escape from the besieged city of Jerusalem, the Edomites captured them and turned them over to the Babylonians! If that were not enough, the prophet notes the Edomites gloated over the tragic demise of Judah! Then when the Babylonians left, they went into Judah to loot and take possession of some of the property!

As we read the book of Obadiah it's hard for us to tell where the anger of the prophet ends and the wrath of God begins. It's likely that Obadiah would see no difference! His vision concentrated on the Lord's judgment. Yet the concern is not just with Edom. The prophet affirms that God's justice extends to all nations, that all people are accountable to the Lord of the universe. But for now, Edom would have its day of reckoning.

For their part, the people of Edom apparently felt safe and secure. Why? Because they dwelt in fortified cities carved into the rocky mountain heights. Thus the prophecy references their soaring with the eagles, their nesting place with the stars! [verse 4] But the prophet realized that though Edom was well prepared militarily and seemingly impregnable, the judgment of the Lord would not be deterred. Even as Obadiah wrote, the Edomites were experiencing expulsion from their own land. Judah, too, had met the Lord's judgment for their sins through national devastation and exile. So God's chosen people were not exempt from divine judgment, though it was to prepare them for greater service.

The tumultuous times in which Obadiah lived are fogged in the distant past. The modern American reader of this book might be excused for saying it has nothing to do with us. It was a localized prophecy addressing specific events in the last centuries we know as BC. On the other hand, this tiny book is part of sacred Scripture, and for that reason through the centuries persons of faith have found not only historical significance, but spiritual relevance in it as well. Let's see if we can discern why.

1. THE LORD IS SOVEREIGN OVER NATIONS

The affirmation in Obadiah, the truth beyond the particular misfortunes of Edom and Israel, is that all nations and peoples are under the watchful eye of God. Historical events, the rise and fall of empires, are somehow shaped into God's overarching plan. The prophet's vision is not primarily a swooping down of supernatural power against Edom or Judah, but a down-to-earth recognition of the natural fruits of national folly. There are plenty of adversaries waiting for the chance to move in when defenses are weakened or internal discord dulls the common will. The prophet sees this, but in this reality he perceives what others do not. That Almighty God is deeply involved, working out his purposes beyond human understanding.

In our secular and materialistic age we have largely lost sight of any divine engagement in human affairs beyond the individual. But Scripture over and over affirms that the nations are under the sovereignty of God, whether or not they acknowledge this. Divine justice is marching across the pages of human history whether we have the capacity to detect it or not. We Christians in the United States typically think of our nation as under divine authority and sovereignty. "In God we trust," we say on our currency. Fewer and fewer people seem to sign off on this belief, apparently, but within the revered documents of our nation's founding there is the affirmation of a divine Hand at work. God's sovereignty, however, is not limited to this nation. It extends to all nations and peoples of earth. Thus, what we do as a nation, and what others do in their national life, is under the scrutiny of God's will and purpose. Where we uphold divine law, seek to exhibit divine justice, have in our core values divine compassion and care, there we may be sure of divine blessing. Where we falter in those commitments, where we go off the rails morally, ascribe more power to our own fortifications than to the strength of the Lord, "lean on our own understanding" as Scripture puts it [Proverbs 3:5], then we like Edom and Judah and countless other nations throughout history will suffer divine judgment.

This prophetic warning and observation often falls on deaf ears today. Yet the tiny book Obadiah reminds us that God is sovereign. God's will and purpose cannot be thwarted.

2. THE LORD OFFERS SALVATION

A second, more hopeful observation from this book is that ultimately those faithful to God will be restored. "Those who have been saved shall go up to Mount Zion," the prophet declares as he speaks for God. "And the kingdom shall be the Lord's." [verse 21] Ezra, Isaiah and

Joel, among others, spoke of a remnant of God's people. [Ezra 9:8; Isaiah 1:9; Joel 2:32] From our New Testament perspective, the apostle Paul echoed that conviction with regard to the Israel of his day, referencing the experience of the prophet Elijah whom the Lord assured there was a cadre of faithful folks who had not "bowed the knee to Baal." [1 Kings 19:18] The Lord God offers salvation to those who will trust in him. We know this supremely through the life and work of Jesus Christ. [Cf., Romans 10:9]

For Obadiah, the restoration of a remnant in Israel meant the re-possession of confiscated lands and the establishment of God's rule on Mount Zion. That attitude was surely behind the disciples' question of the Lord Jesus before he ascended into heaven: 'Will you at this time restore the kingdom to Israel?' [Acts 1:6] That messianic hope suffused much of the religious thinking of Jesus' day. Yet the salvation that came through him was not the establishment of an earthly kingdom. 'My kingdom is not of this world,' he said to Pontius Pilate. [John 18:36] It was a salvation for a Kingdom far greater and deeper than the nationalistic dreams of Obadiah and others. It is a salvation of grace offered to those who trust in the Lord Jesus Christ.

3. THE VICTORY IS THE LORD'S

The prophet did recognize that the victory belonged to God alone, and not to the people. The restoration he envisioned brought great benefits to the people, but ultimately the reign that would be established was God's. Obadiah's closing affirmation was, "The kingdom shall be the Lord's." And this declaration was taken up centuries later in the resounding New Testament hymn: "The kingdom of the world has become the kingdom of our Lord and of his Christ." [Revelation 11:15] I can't hear these words without recalling the majestic strains of Handel's "Messiah." What a triumphal pronouncement!

For Obadiah, and for us, the golden cord of human history binding all things together is the assurance that the Lord God is sovereign. Ultimately God's goodness, justice, mercy, grace and love will prevail over the forces of evil. As Martin Luther's great hymn "A Mighty Fortress Is Our God" says it, "His Kingdom is forever."

JONAH - RELUCTANT REPRESENTATIVE

The word of the Lord came to Jonah a second time, saying, 'Get up, go to Nineveh, that great city, and proclaim to it the message that I tell you.

When God saw what they did, how they turned from their evil ways, God changed his mind about the calamity that he had said he would bring upon them; and he did not do it. Jonah 3:1-2, 10

Some people are just not worth saving! At least that's what the prophet Jonah thought. The Lord had told him to go to the city of Nineveh, the great Assyrian stronghold, and warn them to repent of their evil. But Jonah wasn't keen on that idea. Those wicked Ninevites were the sworn enemies of Israel. Located on the east bank of the Tigris River in what came to be known as the Fertile Crescent, Nineveh was one of the largest cities of the ancient world. Today the city of Mosul, Iraq is in that region. And Jonah knew that Nineveh was a hotbed for all kinds of evil. The Lord knew it, too. God said to Jonah: "Go at once to Nineveh, that great city, and cry out against it; for their wickedness has come up before me." [Jonah 1:2]

I don't know what the conversation between Jonah and Mrs. Jonah was like, but I expect when he told her that the Lord had spoken to him, telling him to get over to Nineveh, she would have said something like, "What, there are no sinners in Israel? What business is Nineveh of yours?" And Jonah figured she had a point. He really had no business going to Nineveh. His life was here in northern Israel. He had gained a bit of a reputation as a religious teacher. People respected him. But he also knew that it wasn't easy to ignore God's calling. Maybe if he just got away for a while, let things simmer down. He checked with the local travel agent and was told that the farthest place from Nineveh (or Israel for that matter) that anyone knew about was Tarshish. If he got on a boat at Joppa, near modern Tel Aviv, he would have to sail westward the length of the Mediterranean Sea before getting to Tarshish in southwestern Spain. The end of the world, by accounts of the Phoenician sailors. 'Sounds good,' he thought, as he bought a ticket.

This old Bible story is a favorite of Sunday school kids. They enjoy hearing about a man of God who tries to get away from the Lord. They get a charge out of hearing about the storm at sea, and Jonah falling asleep on the boat in the middle of the storm, and finally the ship's crew – after realizing that Jonah was fleeing from God – tossing him overboard in the hope of calming the waves. But the most fascinating thing about the story is that big fish the Lord sent to swallow the prophet! We usually think of it as a whale, because that's the biggest sea creature, and any way you look at it, this is a whale of a story! The Bible doesn't say it was a whale, though, and we have the sense that the Lord provided a special marine creature for transporting the prophet where he wanted him to go, slogging along in its innards for three days and three nights. "Then the Lord spoke to the fish, and it spewed Jonah out upon dry land." [Jonah 2:10] And that's where our Scripture lesson today picks up the story.

1. GRUDGING OBEDIENCE

God says to Jonah, 'Now that I have your attention, let me remind you of what you're to do. Go to Nineveh, like I said, and proclaim the message I give you.' Now the reluctant representative of the Lord headed out. But Jonah was a grumbler. Part of his problem was, Jonah knew that the Lord was gracious, slow to anger, abounding in steadfast love, ever ready to relent from punishment. [4:2] So he was suspicious that the main reason he was being sent to Nineveh was not to see the city destroyed, but to provide a way for the people to be saved from destruction. And some people are just not worth saving!

It's one of those stories that captivates us by its very improbability. It stretches the imagination, and that's what engages us. But the truth is, it illustrates in a most telling fashion the reality of God's redemptive purpose, God's unrelenting grace offered to a troubled world. So we are delighted to read that, upon hearing the prophet's message, the people of Nineveh believed God and repented of their evil ways. We are delighted, right?

Jonah wasn't particularly excited about this turn of events. When at last he came grudgingly into the city, he shared no credentials with anyone, did not ask for an audience with the king, did not tell anyone where he was from, gave no introduction to the sacred Torah, nothing. He just walked about a third of the way into the city and cried out, "Forty days more, and Nineveh shall be overthrown." [3:4] He said nothing to the people about turning away from sin and believing in God. He gave no hint that there was the possibility of mercy and forgiveness, that the city might actually be spared. He just pronounced judgment and headed for the hills outside the city to watch what happened. And when the people repented, and the king made a solemn proclamation enjoining the people to cry out to Almighty God with fasting and prayer, and he saw that the Lord did not rain down fire and brimstone, Jonah was angry.

79

2. THE PROPHET'S CONVERSION

When you think about it, the book of Jonah is as much about the conversion of Jonah as it is the repentance of Nineveh. Here is God's man, dutifully (albeit reluctantly) sharing God's message with people, but in his heart of hearts, he didn't want to see Nineveh spared. 'That's what I was afraid of!' he muttered. 'That's exactly why I took that ship to Tarshish. I knew the Lord would do something like this!'

Pouting, Jonah takes up residence on a barren hilltop. He made a little lean-to for shelter, but it wasn't much good. Then, the Lord allowed a large bush to grow over the spot to give greater shade in the heat of the day. This pleased the old prophet, but unfortunately the bush died the next day, and he was exposed to the scorching heat once more. 'I wish I was dead,' said Jonah. Then the Lord spoke to Jonah. And I don't know if you will agree with me, but there is in this divine response something similar to that parable we know as the Prodigal Son. For there were two sons in that story, and both were prodigal, you might say. And the father, displaying a divine "prodigal" love, spoke to the eldest: 'Your brother who was lost is found.' (Luke 15:32) In a way it's reminiscent of the Lord's comment to Jonah. 'You cared about that little shrub, but why do you begrudge my concern for this great city?'

3. ONE OF JESUS' FAVORITES

The story of Jonah was one of Jesus' favorites, too. It was a story he specifically referred to. When he was responding to the taunting of the Pharisees, he said: 'This generation wants a sign from me to prove I am from God. But you will receive no sign except the sign of Jonah.' [Matthew 12:38] He was, we know, citing particularly the fact that Jonah survived those three days in the belly of the fish, and predicting that he himself would be raised from death. [Matthew 12:40] Yet I think there was something else going on, too. The Pharisees were a little like Jonah of old. They were devout, strict believers in the one true God. But they weren't sure anyone else was worth saving. Since they had the inside track on spiritual things, they weren't too concerned about anyone else. In fact, they could see all kinds of reasons why God should destroy all those other wicked folks. Some of Jesus' disciples had a tinge of that attitude, too. [Luke 9:54]

4. US AND THEM

One of the great challenges for the community of faith is to deal with the "us vs. them" mentality. Believers tend to think rather

80

condescendingly of non-believers. That doesn't contribute favorably to our witness for the gospel. The society in general is plagued with the problem, too. We've just come through a turbulent political season with parties bitterly pitted against each other, conservatives blasting liberals, liberals giving conservatives down the river, and rancor from all sides the rule of the day. I've heard otherwise kind and gracious Christian people spout viciousness and hatred on social media and elsewhere, believing somehow they were championing a righteous cause. We had a 'peaceful transition of power,' if you can call a Capitol that is an armed camp peaceful. Unless we're careful, we can fall into the trap of thinking that those who are different from us are just not worth saving! It might even grate on our nerves to be reminded of the gospel message of grace and hope.

In the early weeks of the pandemic, we may have bristled at the notion that some jobs are essential and others aren't. Does that mean some people are not essential? No one would have said so, but there was an itchy implication that seemed to undermine the personhood of many folks. Thankfully we are beyond that.

Jesus did not draw the distinctions between people that the Pharisees and others did. They thought of sinners as being beyond the pale. The fact that Jesus spent time with known miscreants convinced them that he was not a true prophet! [Luke 7:39] Look at Jonah, for instance. He surely had no use for the Ninevites. The Lord Jesus was constantly criticized for his interaction with those considered unworthy by the super religious. He said, however, that he came to seek and save the lost. [Luke 19:10] That's where he was much different from Jonah. The old prophet wanted nothing to do with the sinful people of Nineveh, but Jesus went to supper with such folks as the hated tax collectors, even had one of them in his disciple band. [Mark 2:15-17] He spent time with sinners, the Bible says, and the common people heard him gladly. [Mark 12:37]

You can't read the Gospels without realizing that Jesus saw people in a different way than most of us do. We like to categorize people, but Jesus resisted that idea. When he saw a person like Levi, or Mary Magdalene, or Zacchaeus, or Peter, or Martha, he saw someone who was worth saving. They weren't perfect; they had their issues. Maybe they weren't as far gone as those folks in Nineveh, but probably few of their neighbors would have thought a person like Jesus should regard them as special. But he did.

God sees people differently. Samuel learned that lesson when he was sent to anoint a new king for Israel. The most likely candidates were rejected by the Lord. The least likely one, young David, was selected, because the Lord looks upon the heart. [1 Samuel 16:7] Jonah learned that lesson, too. When he looked at the great city of Nineveh, all he could think about was how wonderful it would be to see it go up in flames! But God saw people worth saving.

So the Scripture tells us that at just the right time, God sent his Son to die for the ungodly. [Romans 5:6] God sent Jesus to save those who seemed not worth saving! And it's a good thing, too. That's how <u>we</u> got grace!

HAGGAI'S HOUSE OF HOPE

The latter splendor of this house shall be greater than the former, says the Lord of hosts. Haggai 2:9

With the rest of the world I was shocked at the news of the devastating fire that destroyed much of the Cathedral of Notre Dame in Paris April 15, 2019. Initially it was uncertain as to whether or not the structure was sound enough to consider restoration, but now, after donations in excess of a billion dollars, the re-build is well underway in hopes of having the church complete by the time the Olympics are played in Paris in 2024. The great gothic cathedral had withstood the ravages of time since its consecration in 1189 AD, including two world wars, the French Revolution's angry mobs and the ensuing Reign of Terror, and many other conflicts. But it almost succumbed to a fire whose origin appears to have been faulty wiring near the roof. Today miles of scaffolding support the reconstruction effort, with over two hundred workers involved in it daily.

Although I have discovered no French lineage in my family tree, am not a Roman Catholic, and have never been to Paris, I was deeply saddened by the near-destruction of the gothic shrine. What a role it has played in the history of that nation! Napoleon Bonaparte crowned himself Emperor there in 1804. Kings and potentates have worshiped in its sacred halls, together with ordinary French citizens who clung to their faith despite harsh governmental sanctions against the church and its clergy. I am aware that in these modern times French Catholicism is but a shadow of its former participation, yet the towers and massive stained glass windows remained an integral part of the soul of the people. So it is encouraging to see progress in the restoration of the building.

It is in light of this contemporary reconstruction project that we may think about the challenge of rebuilding the Temple in Jerusalem that began in 520 BC, over twenty-five hundred years ago. You recall that the city had been sacked by the Babylonians in 586 BC, the Temple was razed, and thousands of people were led away into Babylonian exile. Some seventy years later the Persians had conquered Babylon, and in 538 BC King Cyrus permitted the Judeans to return to their homeland if they wished to do so. The returnees were led by two great Old Testament characters, Ezra and Nehemiah, along with another dynamic personality from the exile named Zerubbabel, a descendant of King David. During the reign of the Persian Darius I, two of the prophets of the Book of Twelve (the Minor Prophets) commenced their ministries: Zechariah and Haggai. It is to Haggai that we turn our attention today.

1. NAMED BUT UNKNOWN

As is true of some of the other prophets, we have no biographical information about Haggai. His name is related to the Hebrew word for festival, so some have conjectured that he may have been born on or around a religious feast day, but that cannot be confirmed. The book of Ezra says simply that Haggai and Zechariah, son of Iddo, prophesied to the Jews who were in Judah and Jerusalem in those years after the return from exile. [Ezra 5:1] Actually, Haggai's prophetic activity occurred over a period of less than four months, according to the book itself. His work began in the second year of King Darius' rule, on the first day of the sixth month, calling on Zerubbabel and the people to begin the task of rebuilding the Temple.

By the twenty-fourth day of that month his message had begun to bear fruit! This is astonishing in itself. There was no social media, no television and radio, no printing press. How did Haggai get his message out? How were the people so inspired and mobilized by his words that Governor Zerubbabel and the people of the city set everything else aside and went to work? Did he march through the streets, declaring in a loud voice that while the people now had managed to erect fine homes for themselves, the house of the Lord still lay in ruins? Did he find a perch on the newly finished city wall from which to proclaim that the people had sown little but harvested much, that while they have clothing no one is warm, and the wages they receive are put into pouches with holes in them? Was a chariot made available to him so he could carry his message across the city? We are not told how he went about his prophetic duties, but whatever method he used, it was effective! By the twenty-fourth day of the ninth month the foundation of the Temple had been laid. But at that point Haggai's prophetic work ended and we do not know if he lived to see the completion of the new Temple.

2. A PROJECT RESUMED

The initial stages of the Temple's reconstruction took place soon after the first returnees arrived in Jerusalem. An altar was built and the Levites established regular services. But the project stalled in the face of outside adversaries, notably the Samaritans and Syrians. It was not resumed until eighteen years later at the behest of the prophet named Haggai we're thinking of today. "You have looked for much, and, lo, it came to little," cried the prophet. "Why? says the Lord of hosts. Because my house lies in ruins, while all of you hurry off to your own houses." [1:9]

It is not possible for us today to relate to the emotions that must have surrounded the rebuilding of the Temple in Jerusalem. Solomon's

Temple had been destroyed and Mount Zion had stood decimated and vacant for over two generations. It had been a national symbol, not simply a religious center but the core of the national life. The conventional wisdom at the time of Jeremiah, before the fall of Jerusalem, was that the Temple could never be destroyed, because it was where the glory of the Lord was found. But that was before the Babylonians came knocking. The years of exile created a spiritual crisis as well as a national and economic one. One Psalm sorrowfully portrays the moment: 'We hung our harps on the willow trees, for our captors demanded of us a religious song. But how could we sing the Lord's song in a foreign land?' [Psalm 137:2-4] It was a Trail of Tears sadly presaging the one in Native American history. With the support of prophets during the exile, though, the Jews in Babylon would learn a new way of worship, and create marvelous documents telling the story of their faith that found their way into sacred Scripture. But the Temple was gone.

They had fared well enough without it back in Babylon. There were other priorities now that they had come back to Jerusalem. After all, very few of them remembered anything about the former glory of the city and its Temple. Evidently there were some who did remember, though. When the foundation of the Second Temple was laid, the word of the Lord came to Haggai, instructing him to speak to Zerubbabel and the people. "Who is left among you that saw this house in its former glory? How does it look to you now? Is it not in your sight as nothing?" [2:3] Those who remembered must have been quite elderly! But Ezra, too, tells us there were some present who remembered. And they wept when comparing the much smaller footprint of the foundation to what they remembered of Solomon's Temple. [Ezra 3:12] But the occasion was joyous nonetheless. The city, the nation, the people were on the way back! They would have a long way to go, and never again would the Temple know the glory it once had.

During the time of Christ the Temple was being rebuilt again. In the years before the Roman rule of Palestine, the Seleucids under Antiochus IV Epiphanes had desecrated the Temple. Herod the Great had started a renovation and expansion project for the Temple in the years before Jesus was born, so that in his lifetime it was known as Herod's Temple. It had been under construction for over forty years when the Lord told his followers that the temple would be destroyed, and in three days be raised again! [John 2:19-22] Of course, he spoke of his own body. But the Temple itself was in fact destroyed by the Romans in 70 AD. Only the western wall, the "Wailing Wall," stands today.

The Gospels tell of Jesus' momentous visits to the Temple in Jerusalem, beginning with his dedication to God as an infant, and then his surprising stopover at age twelve. As an adult, according to the Gospel of John, Jesus came to the Temple early in his ministry, though the other Gospels concentrate his work there during the last week or so of his life.

[Cf., John 7:14; Luke 19:47] It was the scene of some his most dramatic activities, including driving out the moneychangers from the Temple. Quoting Scripture he said, 'My house shall be called a house of prayer, and you have made it a den of robbers!' [Mark 11:15] In the Temple, too, he noticed the widow casting her last coins into the treasury box. [Mark 12:42] His parable of the tax collector and the Pharisee was set in the Temple. [Luke 18:10] The Temple was a major symbol of the religious life of the people in Jesus' day, but he revealed his full authority over it time and again.

Haggai had lit a fire under the people and the Lord's house was moving from dream to reality once more. But there had been disillusionment across the board with the resumption of life in Jerusalem. The early years had seen economic stress, armed conflict with neighbor nations, bitterness between the returnees and those whose families had not been deported but had remained in Palestine all this time. The Temple was just one more evidence of the disconnect between what had been and what now was. But now Haggai's tone changed. Instead of harping on the people to start building that Temple, now he heard the Lord utter a completely new idea.

"Take courage, all you people of the land, says the Lord; work, for I am with you, says the Lord of hosts." [2:4] Haggai reminded the people that Almighty God had brought their ancestors out of Egypt with a promise, and God was still bringing that promise to fruition. "I will fill this house with splendor, says the Lord of hosts... The latter splendor of this house shall be greater than the former, says the Lord of hosts." [2:9]

3. GOD'S HOUSE IS A HOUSE OF HOPE

God's house was to be a house of hope. Unlikely as it must have seemed at the time, the Lord was doing marvelous things! The Second Temple, we are sure, never exceeded the first in terms of its physical appearance. But reading this story we realize that the Lord wasn't talking about a building of cedar and stone. That Temple just prefigured the true Temple that was to come.

Fast-forward to that day not long after the first Christian Pentecost when a young man named Stephen was accused of saying that Jesus would destroy the Temple of his day. When arrested, he was finally given an opportunity to speak. And did he speak! He recounted the history of Israel from the time of Abraham and the patriarchs to Moses and at last to Solomon and his Temple. "Yet the Most High does not dwell in houses made with human hands!" cried Stephen, quoting the prophet Isaiah. [Acts 7:48] The New Testament affirms that in Christ, God has come to "tabernacle" with us. God's Spirit dwells in us, and we who trust in Jesus are the temple of the Lord! [1 Corinthians 3:16]

86

The tabernacle in the wilderness, the Temples of Jerusalem, the great houses of worship located around the world, and this very sanctuary today all point to the same reality. God is faithful and will dwell with his people! With the ancient Haggai we can say, God's house is a house of hope!

ZECHARIAH - PRISONER OF HOPE

Return to your stronghold, O prisoners of hope; today I declare that I will restore to you double. Zechariah 9:12

My sermon file from the Old Testament book of Zechariah is mighty thin. But I have made reference to the Book almost annually, because part of the passage just read this morning is cited in the Gospel account of Christ's triumphal entry into Jerusalem on the first Palm Sunday. The disciples knew their Bible, and when they saw the Master astride a donkey riding through the city gates, they remembered this ancient prophecy from Zechariah: 'Rejoice, daughter of Zion! Your king comes to you righteous and victorious, riding on a donkey.' [Cf., Matthew 21:5] Today, though, is not Palm Sunday, and it's likely that this portion of Scripture would not have occurred to me if it had not been the recommended lectionary selection from the Old Testament this week. Even so, I admit that I had some difficulty deciding to focus on this passage. Apart from the obvious connection with Palm Sunday for us Christians, I didn't see much food for thought in this Scripture reading. Then I stumbled across the phrase in verse 12 that suggested the title of this message, "prisoners of hope." But that was an apparent contradiction, because to be a prisoner is to be confined against one's will, and to have hope is to anticipate release from some sort of problem. The two ideas don't seem to go together, except of course as you realize the prophets often used poetic language to express the Word of God.

Then, as I discussed the matter with my wife Janie, a couple of other poetic references came to me. I recalled the refrain of one of Bob Dylan's songs: "I see my light come shining, from the west down to the east. Any day now, any day now, I shall be released." That, surely, is expressive of a prisoner's hope, isn't it? Then a line from the hymn "Great Is Thy Faithfulness" came to me: "Thy own dear presence to cheer and to guide; Strength for today, bright hope for tomorrow, blessings all mine and ten thousand beside." [Thomas O. Chisolm] The notion that God is our companion, providing strength for our daily needs and hope for an eternal future, pegs the gospel way for many of us.

Soon other biblical ideas crowded in. I thought of Paul writing about hope in Romans. 'Character produces hope, and hope does not disappoint,' he wrote. [Romans 5:5] Abraham, he said, 'in hope believed against hope,' accepting the divine promise that he should be the father of nations. [4:18] In the same letter Paul asks 'the God of hope' to fill his readers with all joy and peace in believing. [15:13] And in that famous chapter 13 of First Corinthians the apostle declares that faith, hope and

88

love abide – noting of course that the greatest of these is love. [1 Corinthians 13:13] Still, that puts faith and hope in pretty good company! Another oft-quoted verse is from First Peter: "Always be prepared to make a defense to any one who calls you to account for the hope that is in you." [3:15]

In further conversation about this, Janie called my attention to one of the devotionals in this past week's readings from the devotional booklet "These Days," which some of you may have seen. We don't often talk about my sermon topics, but because we were planning that she would be with me at church today – a first since her stroke in January-- the matter came up. She's a far more faithful reader of the devotional guide than I am, and she noticed that Zechariah 9:9-12 was the textual foundation for Wednesday's devotional, "Choosing Hope," by Patrick D. Heery. I had already decided to work on this passage, but that cinched it! If Patrick (whom I've never met) thought it was worth exploring, who am I to demur?

1. THE WATERLESS PIT

A little research on the prophet Zechariah offers the surprising information that his public career was a short one, about two years, from 520 to 518 BC. He was a contemporary of another prophet whose work appears in our Bible, Haggai, and they shared some of the same concerns, notably the need to rebuild the temple in Jerusalem, a task that was completed in 516 BC. It may be that Zechariah had this interest because he was descended from the priestly tribe of Levi, though whether or not he actually served as a priest is not known. The situation in Jerusalem and its environs had been tough since the return of the first exiles from Babylon, one of whom was Zechariah's grandfather, Iddo. Those who were part of that first returning group did so in part to try to make a better life in their historic homeland. Not everyone came back, though. Quite a number of the exiles fared well in Babylon and were not interested in going back to Palestine. It soon became apparent that life would not be easy in Jerusalem. The city would have to be rebuilt from the ground up. Houses, infrastructure, public buildings, even the holy temple itself had been utterly destroyed when the Babylonian army crushed Judah. The rebuilding project would be long and hard.

It must have been a source of disillusionment for those returnees that progress toward restoration would take so long and be so hard. The careers of Ezra and Nehemiah, somewhat later, indicate the hardships the people were still suffering, and their susceptibility to the attack of enemies, since the protective wall of Jerusalem had yet to be completed. So in our passage for today, the first use of the word "prisoners" appears in the Lord's assurance to the people because of his everlasting covenant, saying,

89

"I will free your prisoners from the waterless pit." [verse 11] The image of a waterless pit is much more like what we ordinarily would associate with the hopelessness of prison than the follow-up image of "prisoners of hope."

Evidently in Jerusalem at that time there were plenty of people who could be described as 'prisoners of <u>hopelessness</u>.' They did not remember the splendor of Judah before its fall, but from the descriptions passed on to them they knew it was very different from the current reality! For them, the re-establishment of their homeland seemed an arduous and unfulfilling obligation. Some measure of economic relief had been attained, but they had a long way to go. People could barely make it, and here were these holy men like Zechariah tattering on about rebuilding the temple!

I've just read a new biography of Ernest Hemmingway, one of the preeminent American writers of the twentieth century. He was a person of amazing personal gifts and charisma, apparently, a voice for a generation between the two World Wars. But despite his globetrotting lifestyle, his adventures on safari and deep sea fishing, his literary triumphs, his legendary love life, he was beset by many demons. In the end, he took his own life, as had his father before him. He was, in a way of speaking, a prisoner of despair.

In this, he was not alone. There are many people today living in the waterless pit of hopelessness. The pages of our newspaper, the reports of the evening news, often must focus on the tragic tales of people who have gone off the rails emotionally and committed terrible acts of violence. But beyond those sensational events, there are untold multitudes living in the throes of a hopelessness that sees no light at the end of the tunnel.

I don't do much with social media, but the other day a tweet from a friend caught my eye. It was the image of a Post-It note with two words in magic marker. The first was "despair," and a line crossed it out. Below it was the word "hope." While I relate to the message, I also realize that the journey from despair to hope isn't as easy as crossing a word out or flipping a switch! There are an estimated 15 million adult Americans suffering from clinical depression, 6.7% of the population. Additionally, there are untold multitudes self-medicating with alcohol, substance and prescription abuse. Depression in its various forms is a complicated and painful experience for the sufferer and loved ones. My mother was bipolar, and the disorder was more prevalent later in her life. She responded well to medication, but sometimes when she started to feel better, she would neglect to take her medicine, which often is a characteristic of the disease. Perhaps you have known of similar situations. The point here is that for individuals, communities and nations, the "waterless pit" is a tough place to be!

Yet if we listen to the prophet's message, the Lord God Almighty is coming to the rescue! That's what that picture of the king riding into the city on a donkey is to convey. Here is the one who will bring peace,

90

establish justice, and release the prisoners from the waterless pit! We can't help remembering that when our Lord spoke at his home synagogue in Nazareth, he quoted from the Book of Isaiah who proclaimed the Messiah would bring release to the captives. Jesus Christ came into the world to break the bonds of sin and death, the prison of despair. Those who welcome him find genuine hope.

2. PRISONERS OF HOPE

Having considered the bleak portrayal of prisoners in the waterless pit, we turn now to that other phrase that speaks of a different kind of captivity, "prisoners of hope." There is scarcely a more negative term than the word "prisoner." It denotes the loss of freedom, separation from home and community, physical and psychological pain and deprivation. In 2013 there were some 2.2 million adults in prisons and jails in the United States, and no doubt the number is even higher today. To use language like "prisoners of hope" is not intended to minimize the terrific challenge our society is facing in its justice system for the protection and welfare of the public, and for the rehabilitation of those who, having served their time, must re-enter society. But the phrase is the prophet's bold and divinely inspired metaphor for the release God's people receive from the Lord. No longer are we to be imprisoned in walls of guilt, hatred, prejudice, greed, self-centeredness and disbelief. Now we are liberated into the loving care of the Heavenly Father, for in sending his Son into the world, he has paid the cost of our freedom. Without the saving intervention of Christ, we are still hopelessly imprisoned by sin and death. But because of him, we are pardoned and set free, prisoners now to a living hope in Christ!

3. OUR HOPE IS IN CHRIST

There is such a thing as false hope. People sometimes warn us about this. But the gospel is not about false hope. It is hope based on truth, and for that reason, as Paul affirmed, it will not disappoint. The truth is made known in Jesus Christ. Our hope is in him.

When the apostle Paul stood before the tribunal in Jerusalem, he declared: "I stand on trial because of the hope of the resurrection of the dead," referring to the resurrection of Christ but also to our hope of resurrection in him. [Acts 23:6] Paul was a prisoner of hope, the hope that is real in Christ Jesus.

Psalm 42 has a repeated verse that says well what I'm speaking of today. "Why are you cast down, O my soul, and why are you disquieted within me? Hope in God; for I shall again praise him, my help and my God." [Ps 42:5, 11] Our hope is not in ourselves, not in the fickle circumstances of life, not even in other people who mean so much to us. No, our hope is in God alone, through Jesus Christ. When we surrender to him, it is as if we are prisoners in God, but there is no freedom in the world like it! For then we are, like Zechariah and his countrymen, prisoners of hope!

PARABLES

THE NEIGHBOR

But wanting to justify himself, he asked Jesus, 'And who is my neighbor?' Luke 10:29

Teachers know that one way students learn is by asking questions. In fact, a teacher often can detect the student's level of understanding the subject matter by the way he or she asks a question about it. I've been in situations where I felt I didn't even know enough to ask a decent question! There are questions, then, that are asked for the sake of gaining information.

Some questions, though, are asked from a different motive. They don't arise from a desire for information but rather are designed to impress the teacher (and other students) with one's knowledge. In this case the questioner is looking for recognition, for praise. That's not all bad, of course, but it's not quite the same as seeking knowledge. It's a way of showing off the knowledge we already have.

Then there's a kind of question that's intended to embarrass or trip up the instructor, a question posed for intimidation. It's the kind of question that lures one into a trap: if you give one answer, you may offend this particular group, but give another answer and you risk offending another group. If you've had to field a loaded question like that, maybe you've had a taste of what Jesus must have felt frequently when he was dealing with so many different kinds of people. Some of these folks meant him no good at all, and were eager to see him discredited in the eyes of the public. So again and again in the Gospels we read of someone asking a question of Jesus that is really not for information at all, but artfully crafted to undermine Christ's authority.

1. AN INNOCENT QUESTION?

That's what happened in our lectionary reading from the Gospel of Luke today when a man who was an expert in the religious law asked Jesus what he must do to inherit eternal life. On the surface of it, you might think this was a perfectly innocent question. And you may be inclined to give the questioner the benefit of the doubt, because he at least had the good sense to ask Jesus about such a matter! Unfortunately there are many people who go through life with that kind of question in their hearts, but never get around to asking Jesus about it. But as you know, when something is said, often there is meaning conveyed beyond the words themselves. For instance, in this story the man who asked this question first 'stood up' in the midst of the crowd, that is, he wanted Jesus (and everyone else) to notice him. We further have the sense that there was something in the way he spoke, something in his manner or some gesture that gave away his insincerity. Because right away the Gospel writer inserts the editorial comment that this question was asked to 'test' Jesus. To put Christ on the spot, to potentially embarrass and ridicule him. But Jesus was not taken in. He knew this man was a teacher of the law, and so he threw the subject back to him. 'What is written in the law? How do you read it?' Jesus had turned the tables. But now the man puffs up with pride, because he believes he knows the answer! He's going to make a hundred on this test, he can feel it! Everyone will be amazed at his comeback. Quoting the Bible, he says, 'You shall love the Lord your God with all your heart, soul and strength and your neighbor as yourself.' [Deuteronomy 6:5; Leviticus 19:18] Now those of you who are Bible scholars will realize that in Matthew's account of this episode, it is Jesus who answers with this great Summary of the Law. But here in Luke these words are on the lips of the scribe. Grinning smugly, he seems to be saying, 'Top that!'

Jesus, nodding in agreement, simply says, 'You're right, do this and you will live.' That would ordinarily have been the end of the matter, and we think that perhaps Jesus was ready to leave. But this man wasn't satisfied. He hadn't achieved his purpose. He decides to go one better. 'Well, then, just who is my neighbor?' he asks. Of course we know from our experience with this fellow already that he wasn't interested in information. And since his attempt to impress fell flat, he was going for something more. He wanted to justify himself, to make himself look good, to have the last word, so to speak. This question about a neighbor was bound to trip up this teacher from Nazareth, "nowheresville" to the scribe's way of thinking. But to his surprise, and perhaps that of others gathered nearby, Jesus just told a story. It's a story that has been woven into the fabric of human consciousness ever since, the parable we know as the Good Samaritan.

2. THE STORY

It is such a profound and graphic story that almost anyone, even the non-church-goer, could give you the gist of it. A man traveling alone down the treacherous and steep road leading to Jericho was mugged by thieves, beaten and left for dead in the ditch at the side of the road. After a while a man dressed in the priestly robes of the temple came along, but when he saw the wounded man in the ditch, he hurried to the other side of the road and passed on by. A little later, a second man, also a notable in the religious establishment, a temple official called a Levite, came on the scene. But he too skirted around and moved on down the road without stopping to render aid. Finally, a third man came along. He was not dressed in fine robes. He had no position of religious authority. He was not even a true

96

Israelite! He was an outsider, a half-breed, a Samaritan of all things! But this man, seeing the one in the ditch, got off his beast, tended the hurt man's wounds as best he could, then lifted him onto the donkey and brought him down to the town. When they arrived, the Samaritan found an inn – the closest thing there was to an emergency room! He told the innkeeper to care for the man, paying up front. He asked that the manager put all expenses on his tab, promising that he would pay any additional costs upon his return.

It's an amazing story. And Jesus concludes it with a question of his own: 'Which of these three proved neighbor to the one who was robbed?' Then the lawyer spoke up in answer, perhaps less enthusiastically this time, saying, 'The one who showed mercy.' By the way, he didn't even acknowledge that the rescuer was a Samaritan. Jesus turned a searching eye upon him, a glance that brooked no further discussion, and said, 'Go and do likewise.'

The question for Jesus wasn't who is my neighbor, but who am I neighbor to? The question isn't who do I <u>not</u> have to love as myself – which is what the lawyer wanted to know – but rather who will need my love and care at any given moment? No doubt the questioner thought Jesus would say, as other teachers might have, your neighbor is the one you can count on, the one who is closest to you in terms of your own interests and values, the like-minded person. Love that person as yourself, because he or she is most like you! Indeed that is the way we often think of neighbors. There are neighbors we like because they are "neighborly," and of course there are others in the neighborhood who may seem less so. The man who asked this question seemed to want Jesus to say, 'Love the people who love you in return; do for those who are able to repay you.' But that's not the way Jesus saw it. For him, the question had to do with who we need to neighbor! So if there is one in need, someone who has been robbed and beaten by life, someone who has been victimized by circumstance, that person may well need neighboring from us.

3. RELATING TO THE STORY

That's not the way we hear this parable at first, I don't think. Most of us can relate to the fellow in the ditch to some extent! We probably know what it's like to have an unexpected setback. 'Life comes at you hard,' that old car insurance commercial used to say. And we agree. We are vulnerable to attack – whether from thieves or terrorists or terrible disease. Even if we haven't personally suffered so painfully, we probably know someone who has. It's commonplace in the city where I live to hear news reports of shootings, drunk driving deaths, domestic violence. So when Jesus talked about one who was left for dead by the side of a road, he might

97

just as well have been describing a story from a current newspaper! Sadly, just in the last few days the headlines have again carried stories of black men killed in police custody in Louisiana and Minnesota, and white police officers gunned down in Dallas in apparent retaliation. When will we as a society learn to say, "Enough!"?

We may relate, then, to the victim in the story. Or maybe not. We might find ourselves wondering why this man had used such poor judgment to be travelling on a dangerous road all by himself. There is a tendency in us at times to "blame the victim," don't you think? Yet as much as we may either identify with him or criticize his situation, the story moves beyond him. It talks about those two religious leaders who happened along the road just shortly after the attack. Inexplicably – to our way of thinking – they pass by on the other side. Wait a minute! There's something wrong with this picture, we say. Aren't these two fellows devoted men of God? Indeed, the unreligious person hearing this story is apt to say, 'See, I told you all those church folks are just hypocrites!'

Sometimes to stop and lend a hand means taking a pretty big risk! Today we hear of schemes on the open highway where a would-be Good Samaritan is attacked when trying to help a supposedly stranded motorist. Even if we might not be facing personal risk to help out a friend or acquaintance, at the very least it's an imposition, maybe a costly one. It may involve getting our hands dirty. We don't know what was in the minds and hearts of those two in the story who went by on the other side. Maybe they were afraid of being attacked themselves. Maybe they were simply on a tight schedule and couldn't be delayed. Maybe superiors had warned them against taking too long on the trip. Whatever the cause, the glaring fact is that these two representatives of the religious world went by on the other side.

Now we can probably relate to that, too, if we're honest with ourselves. We who are trying to live for God day by day may get nervous when we hear this story again. Because we suspect that there have been times when we could have responded to someone in need, opportunities to help that were within our capacity, but we did not. We meant no harm by it, but we had our own responsibilities, our schedule to meet. Or we might have had some previous experience with this person that taught us not to be vulnerable to them again. Perhaps we were running low on funds ourselves. Whatever! We may have had our conscience gnaw at us for failing to do what we felt we should have done. It's pretty easy to be hard on the priest and Levite in the story because we can't understand their uncaring attitude. That is, until we sense something of that same attitude in ourselves. Like it or not, we probably can relate a little bit to these two who passed by, if only negatively.

The story, I believe, is intended to have this effect on us – first to allow us to sympathize with the victim, then to puzzle over the reaction of two prominent spiritual leaders.

But the story moves on. Here comes the Samaritan man. He, of all people, would not be expected to help a fallen Hebrew man. There was bad blood between the two races. Part of it was theological, each group thinking the other was not quite orthodox enough. Part of it was economic, because the Samaritan was not obliged to follow the same commercial restrictions and pay all the same taxes as the Israelite. Part of it was historical. The Samaritans were the posterity of a fringe of ancient Israel that was not taken into Babylonian captivity, but left to intermarry with neighboring nations and thus have their religious traditions -- and their bloodlines – corrupted. They had lost their cultural identity, as far as Israel was concerned. They were neither Jew nor Gentile, and they were antagonistic toward both. So here comes this Samaritan down the road. Usually, the Hebrew man and the Samaritan man wouldn't even speak if they encountered each other. Rarely would they even do business together. So under these circumstances you would expect that the Samaritan would pass by on the other side. After all, our highest and best did that! This nobody, this non-entity, this outsider, surely he would do no better. In fact, if you listen between the lines of the story, you might hear the twitters in the gathered crowd when Jesus mentions the Samaritan. But the Master presses on toward an astonishing outcome. The Lord sees this questioning scribe and his ilk as the religious elite of the society – not unlike the two men in the parable, the cream of the crop, spiritually speaking. But notice how they stack up against this quiet Samaritan!

4. THERE'S SOMETHING ABOUT THAT SAMARITAN

Now you can hear some bitter gnashing of teeth in the back of the crowd when Jesus finishes his story! It's a beautiful parable to us, but to those first hearers, it wasn't so nice. It called their whole way of thinking into question. Suddenly they were led to see that their religious formality and sense of superiority meant next to nothing when it came to really making a difference for good in the world. These two paragons of religious virtue didn't even lift a finger to help a fallen countryman! But this Samaritan, a traveller on the same road -- the person most of Christ's hearers wouldn't have given the time of day -- look what he did!

At some point you begin to get the feeling that Jesus is saying something important here. There's something about that Samaritan that has a familiar feel to us. Gradually it dawns on us that Jesus himself is a little like that man. He came from an out-of-the-way place, as far as the religious authorities were concerned. He was nobody important, they thought. He was maligned and ridiculed, and even the occasion of this parable was an instance of that effort. But this Stranger from Galilee has indeed reached down to the one in the ditch again and again. He has always had time for the downtrodden and victimized. He has lifted up the fallen one, carried him in his arms like the Good Shepherd carries a little lamb. And finally, Jesus has paid it all! He has paid for all the sin, all the guilt, all the hurt, all the woundedness. Jesus paid it all!

This One who makes himself known to us in the parables is not like us, not really. He doesn't think as we do. His understanding of justice and mercy is different from our own. His perception of life in the Kingdom of God is so distinctive as to seem beyond our grasp. Here is the true Good Samaritan, the genuine Neighbor, walking our dangerous road, noting that humankind has been thrown into the ditch by a vicious Marauder and by our own stumbling and willfulness. He comes off his rightful place of security, chooses to wade into the mire of the ditch, repels the assaults of all who would attack, binds up our wounds, and carries us at last to an eternal abode where all costs have been paid in our behalf.

This is our truest Neighbor, and we have no capacity to repay him, except this: to accept the love he offers, to be healed by his grace, to adopt his perspective on the world rather than to be content with our own, to align ourselves with his cause of reconciliation rather than casting dark glances at those who are not like ourselves. He is the Samaritan who has turned aside to help us. Greater love has no one than this, for this One has laid down his life for us! [John 15:13]

A GLIMPSE OF GRACE

Then Jesus said, 'There was a man who had two sons. Luke 15:11

Families, right? Oh, I know that during holiday seasons like the one we just came through we often pretend that our families don't really have any problems, but even the best of them do from time to time. So when our Lord tells this gripping story of a family in Palestine, we're on all-too familiar turf. Maybe the issues aren't quite so blatant in our own circles of loved ones as they appear to be in this account from Luke 15 -- and we're fortunate if they aren't! – but we at least know of situations where relationships have been pretty strained.

Tradition calls this story the Parable of the Prodigal Son, and it's surely one of the most familiar and beloved of all Christ's parables. It's also the longest parable recorded in the Gospels, five-hundred and nine words of English text in my copy of the Bible. The Lord Jesus, we know, was the greatest storyteller of all, and he was also the master of succinct expression, drawing panoramic word pictures with the simplest phrases. Here in this text it could be said that we get two stories in one, though it's clear from the very outset that the Lord intends this to be a single narrative: "There was a man who had two sons…"

Jesus loved to teach in parables. Depending on your criteria, there are between forty and fifty parables attributed to Christ in the Gospels. They always begin with a situation or experience with which his hearers would have been instantly familiar – a farmer planting his field, a landowner putting his workers in charge while he went on a journey, a woman searching for a lost coin from the cookie-jar. But if the parables start with the familiar, they don't stay there long. Typically there's an unexpected twist, such as the despised Samaritan's care for a man who was mugged, or the decision of the banquet host to send for the poor, the sick and infirm to come to the table. In the parables the Master opens the curtains of everyday routine to let in the sunlight of divine grace again and again. So it is in this story today.

Part of our difficulty in hearing this text is that it's almost too familiar. It's hard to put ourselves in the place of the first hearers of the story. To us the parables are predictable because we've studied them so often. But that was not the case for Christ's initial audiences. What they heard often made them, well, mad.

101

1. TWO ORDINARY PRODIGALS

Doctor Luke does us an editorial favor at the beginning of this chapter, informing us that at this point in Jesus' ministry "the tax collectors and sinners were all drawing near to hear him. And the Pharisees and scribes murmured, saying, 'This man receives sinners and eats with them.'" [Luke 15:1-2] Knowing the reaction of these religious people to his activities with the folks categorized as sinners, Jesus told the three stories we have in this chapter. This one, the Parable of the Prodigal Son, seems to me to be a bit misnamed. There are really two prodigals in the story. And they're both fairly prosaic, ordinary prodigals at that.

The younger son starts the action with a rather bizarre request. He asks his father for his share of the inheritance. We don't hear the gasps in the crowd gathered around Jesus, perhaps, but there were some. This just wasn't done. It was tantamount to wishing his father was dead, this young fellow not wanting to wait to get the cash. This was a strident abuse of the Fifth Commandment that says, "Honor your father and mother." [Exodus 20:12] Passages from the sacred books of Deuteronomy, Numbers and Leviticus provided the relevant legislation regarding inheritance for Hebrew Law. Essentially, the rubric was that the elder son of the family was to receive two-thirds of the father's property at his death, and any younger sons would divide equally the remaining one-third. And though it was not completely unheard of for a landowner to divide his property before death, it was still understood that he retained ultimate control of it as long as he lived. In other words, in a worst-case scenario, an heir might have received the use of a portion of the property, but could not have sold it or otherwise disposed of it until the death of the father. By the way, the ancient commentaries sagely cautioned against parents doing even this much. But here this youth – maybe in early teenage, since he's assumed not to be married – goes way beyond propriety. He wants it, and he wants it now!

Today, all this might not seem so surprising. In modern life there are sometimes good reasons for a person to dispose of property among heirs while still living. But in those days, this request represented a contemptuous insult. Ties to family, village, religion, and above all, land, went deep. One's selfhood was bound up the relationships that meant so much. Who knows what lay behind this boy's demand? Maybe the younger son just simply recognized that he would never amount to anything unless he got out on his own, made his own way in the world. Maybe there had been friction already between the two brothers, something that will crop up again later in the story. Perhaps there was even a disdainful attitude toward his father, a subtle criticism of the way Dad was managing the farm. Could it be that he had heard of opportunities for prosperity in the far country? After all, at the time of Christ there were about four million Jews living in countries other than Palestine, and only a half million in the Holy Land itself. Others had gone to the "far country" too, in search of a new life. Whatever the case, this fellow was ready to give up the security of his father's household, take a cash settlement of approximately one-third of the estate, and head out the door for parts unknown.

Disciples, scribes, Pharisees, tax collectors, all within earshot of the story would by now be totally outraged at this younger son. But Jesus pressed on. Things went from bad to worse for the lad. Once he came to a far country, no doubt a place populated by Gentiles, predictably he squandered everything he had on loose living. It's what the sages had warned might happen. It's what everyone in the household had worried about. As long as the money held out, the youngster was thrilled. But soon it was gone and life got tougher. There was nothing for him to do but find a job, and what he ended up with brought even more muttering among Christ's audience. This young heir of a landed gentleman was now in what was perceived to be an unclean country, working for an unclean farmer, tending unclean animals and wishing for the food they ate! It doesn't get much worse than that for a Jewish boy in the first century.

Unlike the first listeners to this story, we probably have some sympathy for the kid. It's not uncommon for young folks to want to strike out on the own, even to sow a few wild oats. Boys will be boys, right? We agree that this boy made some bad errors in judgment, but there's something about the prodigal. He captures our imagination and we can identify a little with him. We may even feel a little sorry for him. Part of it, no doubt, is that we know the rest of the story. The Bible tells us that when he had hit rock bottom, "he came to himself," in other words, he came to his senses. He'd been living in a fantasy world, and now it had soured beyond belief. Now he was not only a stranger in a strange land, but he was in danger of starving to death alone. And it came to him that those who were hired hands on his father's place were far better off than he was here in the pigsty. He decided that he would get up and go home. But knowing that he couldn't be regarded as a son any more, he devised a speech that might entice his father to employ him. "Father I have sinned against heaven and before you, and am no longer worthy to be called your son. Treat me as one of your hired servants."

Something tells me he didn't bother with a thirty-day notice to his employer. He struck out for home, in rags and barefoot, with nothing to his name. He would sooner face the humiliation of a return in defeat than to continue down a path to oblivion.

The father, it turns out, was waiting for him at the gate, but let's hold that thought for a moment. Let's turn now briefly to the older son, the guy I refer to as the second prodigal.

103

He's the character in the story we love to hate. Have we known our share of these kinds of folks! He is filled with righteous indignation when he finds out that the kid brother has returned, only to be treated as an honored guest at a great feast. He pouts in the barn while everyone else is at the party. Can't you just see him, mucking out the stalls, getting madder with each shovel-full! He feels unjustly treated by the patriarch, thinks that scallywag of a brother got away with it! He's always been suspicious that his parents loved the brat more than they loved him anyway. Chances are, he's thinking about taking a trip to the far country himself, it worked so well for the little guy!

The centuries of artwork focused on this story rarely feature the second son. What captures our imagination is the repentance and return of the first boy. This other guy is just a stick in the mud, a party-pooper.

Yet I have a feeling that as this story unfolded for the first time, some of the listeners recognized in the second son a person of real substance. Here was a young man who was dedicated to duty. He did what he was told, kept his nose clean. The audience probably felt he had every reason to remonstrate with Dad. It's just not fair!

2. AN EXTRAORDINARY FATHER

There are two parts of the story, and the character that is in both parts is the father. It strikes us that the central figure of the parable is not the younger son – though he gets a lot of ink – and certainly not the older one. Neither of these ordinary prodigals commands our attention quite like this most extraordinary father. But if the crowd listening to Jesus was unnerved by the actions of the younger son, and if they were a little empathetic with the perceived mistreatment of the second, they must have been downright aghast at the behavior of the father in the story!

Here again our modern way of thinking doesn't quite grasp the irony in Christ's depiction of this father. The culture of ancient Palestine, like others of the period, was patently patriarchal. The father, especially one wealthy enough to own land, ruled the roost. His children were virtually his property and he could do with them as he pleased. He could give and receive in marriage in their behalf. He determined their future and required their unquestioned obedience. There may have been a little truth to the elder son's comments that he had worked as a slave, obeying all his father's commands. That was the way of the world in those days.

The image of a father watching for a long-lost prodigal would have seemed absurd! And if by chance the young fellow did come home and ask for a job, the typical father would have been within his rights to have him flogged or worse. If such a position were granted, it would be purely probationary. That's the response Christ's first hearers might have expected

104

from the father. But Jesus doesn't tell the story that way. Quite unexpectedly, this unusual father sees the boy afar off and runs to him, falling on his neck and kissing him, he won't even let the youth get out the speech he has prepared!

'Quick! Bring my best robe, the one reserved for our most honored guests. What! No ring? Bring a new ring. And look, you don't have any sandals! Ach, your feet are bleeding. Bring out some shoes,' he cries to his employees. 'And while you're at it, have the kitchen get to work on a feast. We'll have a party, because this son who was lost is found, the one whom we thought dead is alive again!'

Now when this part of the story is shared, you can sense a tension in the listening group. What kind of father is this? Has he no shame? Where is his pride? In fact, in my mind's eye, I think I can see a couple of listeners edging toward the back, maybe they're about ready to leave. One of them looks a little familiar. Not a scribe, no, but is that old Judas there? Maybe.

This father is not like any ordinary father in Palestine then. And to tell the truth, he isn't like most of us modern fathers, either. We'd want to be sure the boy's so-called repentance really sticks! Once burned, shame on you; twice burned, shame on me, we say. Fatted calf indeed!

But our Savior often talked about a different Father, his heavenly Father. The prophet Isaiah noted that 'God's ways are not our ways, nor his thoughts our thoughts.' [55:9] The Bible says that God is ready to pardon sinners, that as far as east is from west, that's how far God puts our transgressions away from us. And as a father pities his children, so the Lord feels for those who fear him. [Psalm 103:12-13]

In this story there is a noticeable absence of a mother in the family. Perhaps she has died, since there is no mention of her. Yet in the clearly expressive response of the father to the returning son, don't we see something of a mother's love? If she were living, we expect she sometimes prodded her husband, asking, 'Have you been down to the gate yet today? Maybe he's coming!' Not like the typical mother and father of the time at all.

Then in the portion of the story dealing with the elder son, we see more evidence of an extraordinary father. This unusual father quite uncharacteristically leaves his guests and goes out to the barn in search of the elder son. By the way, we church folks like to think about God searching for the lost, and certainly that is what Jesus said of himself. [Luke 19:10] But in this story, this father appears to be looking for someone who presumably was already found, someone who never really left home! In reality he was as distant spiritually as if he'd been in a far country. If the young son had abused this father with his insensitive demand for money, then the older son disrespected him with the implication that he was behaving as a fool toward the ne'er-do-well. 'This son of <u>yours</u> has wasted all your property on, well, you know! And by the way, I've worked my fingers to the bone for you and you never even let me have a little party with my friends, to say nothing of this fiasco!' This is the bitterness of a son who feels like nothing more than a servant in his father's house. He's brooded on this for a long time.

With a patience and long-suffering that is unusual in this world, the father approaches the young man in the barn, calling him, "My child." You'd think, wouldn't you, that he would at least be angry at this one. But no, instead he reaffirms that everything that belongs to the father belongs to the son, that he has been with him always and there would never be anything to separate them. Yes, he reminds the boy that his younger brother is home, and it would be "fitting" if he joined the party. But the story is open-ended. The jury is still out on what this self-righteous brother will do.

3. AN EXTRAORDINARY SON

Because the three characters in our story are so absorbing, we may not have noticed that there is another Son in the passage. He is, of course, the Storyteller. Jesus knew human nature to the core, the prodigals in all of us, the hypocrisy and self-justification, the head-strong self-centeredness, our tendency to waste the gifts of God, our capacity to criticize others, to be skeptical when they have experienced a spiritual transformation. He knew it all. So he told these stories to lift a mirror before us.

But he knew something more, something no one else has known in the same way. He knew the character, mind, will and redemptive purpose of the heavenly Father. Jesus reminded his disciples that he did nothing of his own authority. [John 5:30] He came simply to do the will of the Father who sent him. He came to reveal the Father, that is, to show humanity who God the Father really is! The works he did were the works of God; the compassion he showed is the compassion of God; the forgiveness and mercy he extended to sinners (and those who didn't know they were sinners) is the same mercy that flows from the extraordinary heart of the Father. Christ said to Philip: "Have I been with you so long, and yet you do not know me, Philip? He who has seen me has seen the Father!" [John14:9]

This extraordinary Son came down from heaven, sent from the heart of God to a truly far country! 'He came to his own and his own did not accept him.' [John 1:11] But he came to seek and save the lost, to receive sinners and eat with them, to somehow reach out to Pharisee and tax collector, devoted believer and hardened criminal, prodigals and fathers and mothers, brothers and sisters, children and seniors, the sick, the poor and the weak, the rich and powerful. He came for all! And he didn't wait for us to repent or turn our lives around or get right with God. The Bible says that 'God shows his love for us in that while we were yet sinners Christ died for the ungodly!' [Romans 5:6]

In this parable our Savior pulls back the curtain of everyday experience and grants us a glimpse of grace. Yet truly in his life, death and resurrection, all done for our sakes, we see this grace upon grace!

Can you identify with any of the characters in the story? Even more important, have you placed your trust in the Storyteller, Jesus Christ, the true Son of God, through whom we may become children of God, joint heirs of the Kingdom of heaven?

THE SOWER

And he (Jesus) told them many things in parables, saying 'Listen! A sower went out to sow. Matthew 13:3

Several of the parables of Jesus recorded in the Gospels focus on what we might term the "divine agronomy." They are portrayals from the natural world of planting and harvesting, but they take on a larger than life symbolism because they clearly reflect God's perspective on our typical way of thinking. For example, we have the Parable of the Wheat and Tares, in which despite the sowing of good seed, a mixed crop of weeds and grain is produced. [Matthew 13:24-33] There's the Parable of the Vineyard Workers who, though they were hired at different times of the day, all received the same wages, which seems unfair on the surface of it. [Matthew 20:1-16] Christ spoke of the earth producing, "all by itself," with very little involvement of the farmer, once the seed is in the ground. [Mark 4:26-29] He compared the kingdom heaven to a tiny mustard seed planted in the garden that grew into a mighty tree [Luke 13:19]. But in the same chapter of Luke Jesus tells of a man who found no fruit on his fig tree and angrily ordered it to be cut down, only to hear his servant intercede, saying he would continue to work with the tree and see if it would bear next year, if not, it could be cut down. [13:6-9] And then there's today's story of the sower, the seeds and soil, told here in Matthew, but also in Mark [4:1-9] and Luke [8:4-8].

The Palestine of Jesus' day was largely agricultural, so when he wanted to share profound spiritual truth, he offered stories from that rural way of life that would be familiar to most of his hearers. But to be honest, I'm not much of a gardener or farmer. Some people naturally have a green thumb, but I'm not one of them. So I try to find ways to relate to the parable in a somewhat more contemporary scenario. In this case, I'm thinking about lawncare!

My next door neighbors have re-sodded their front lawn this past week. It was a lot of work, scalping and leveling and rolling out the sod and pouring the water to it. But it looks good so far. Recently one night I was having trouble sleeping, and I surfed the TV channels in the hope of finding something that would make me nod off! I saw an infomercial that proclaimed a product that was guaranteed to grow grass even in the toughest spots. Since I have a few bare spots in my lawn, and since I don't really want to put quite as much work in (or spend as much) as my neighbors have, that got my attention. Apparently, all you have to do is spray this product through your ordinary garden hose and, Voila! Up comes the beautiful, lush green grass. To prove how effective this product is, it was sprayed on the back of a park bench, and lo and behold, grass

108

grew so thick you couldn't see the bench. Now I see some incredulous looks as I relate this, yet there may be folks present who have tried this product with good results. I personally don't know if it really works or not, though I admit to being a bit skeptical. Like so many things on TV commercials, it seems too good to be true. It got me thinking, though. If there were such a product in ancient times to make crops grow, do you imagine the sower in the Lord's parable would have used it? I don't think so. That would have destroyed the story.

The parable as we have it from the Master Storyteller portrays a real-life scenario from the Palestine of the first century AD. No doubt Christ's first hearers were thoroughly familiar with the imagery of a farmworker toiling in the sun, broadcasting seed. And certainly they knew the risks inherent in such an enterprise, because some of the seed would simply not produce. Only a portion of the seed would actually take root and grow. But that did not deter the sower. It was just the way things were. His task was to cast seed.

Christ's stories of farms and vineyards were given before the age of mechanization, before the advances of modern agricultural practices. It seems strange to us moderns that seed might be sown *before* the ground was plowed or otherwise prepared. If there was any preparation of the ground before the sower set out to broadcast seed, nothing is mentioned of that. We can take it for granted, though, that Christ's original hearers of the parable knew all that was involved. And even if our own approach to gardening and planting is different, perhaps we can still relate to the sower's limited ability to determine the outcome of all his labor.

Depending on how you define the term parable, there are 57 of them in the Gospels, 26 of which are taken directly from the ordinary everyday life of folks who worked on farms and vineyards. Some of the parables, of course, are duplicated in the three synoptic Gospels, but some are not. Our word parable is based on a Greek term that means to "throw alongside." That suggests to us that a parable is intended as a comparison. Sometimes Jesus made the comparison idea very clear, beginning a thought with, "The kingdom of heaven is like…" Someone has defined a parable as a "glimpse of earthly life with a heavenly meaning." Jesus Christ told heart-reaching stories, little side-glances of human experience that opened the doors of spiritual truth. The late Nobel Prize-winning author and holocaust survivor Elie Wiesel once observed that "God created human beings because he loved stories." Certainly Jesus loved stories, loved to tell them, loved to illustrate peerless truth about God and humankind through them. The images Jesus shared are engraved deep in our culture, especially for church folks like us.

The Parable of the Sower is perhaps not quite as well known as that of the Good Samaritan, or the Pharisee and Publican, or the Lost

Sheep, but it ranks pretty high on the scale of familiar passages. We are aided in our interpretation of the parable because, just a few verses down in this same chapter of Matthew, the Lord himself gives us the meaning. He tells his disciples that the seed is the word of God that is sown among the hearts of people. Because some are not very receptive, that is, they seem hardened to the Good News, the evil one snatches the word away like birds take away seed that falls on the hard-packed earth. Other people appear on the front end to be excited about the word of God, but soon their enthusiasm wanes because, in the image of the parable, they represent rocky ground. The word can't take root there. Then some of the seed falls on thorny ground where the enticements of this world choke it out. But in the end, there is also seed that falls on the receptive, broken and contrite heart. This word takes root and produces an amazing fruitfulness.

Some of you have no doubt studied this parable repeatedly in Bible classes, heard sermons on it over the years. Its truth is still as challenging as ever, and we see the reality of it in day-to-day life. For the moment, though, I will ask your indulgence to think about the parable in a slightly different light.

1. AN AUTOBIOGRAPHICAL REFLECTION

Although the parable clearly is about the various kinds of "soils," and little is actually said about the sower himself, I believe the sower to be crucial to the story. Jesus begins this story with characteristic directness and few details. A sower went out to sow. We aren't told if the sower owns the garden, nor do we know if he is young or old, wealthy or poor. All we know is the sower went out into the field to work. We're given no weather report, no information about the season of the year. The sower just gets to work, broadcasting seed by hand as he strides forth. The fact that this resulted in some seed falling where it couldn't produce well doesn't mean there was any carelessness on the part of the sower. He was doing his best, taking care of responsibilities to be the best of his ability. You might think of this parable almost in autobiographical terms for Jesus. Christ himself is the bringer of the seed of the gospel. In his Person he is the Word of God sent into the world. As he shared his message, he noted the antagonism of many, the indifference of others, and even the fickle enthusiasm of fair-weather disciples. But there were those handpicked few who, warts and all, followed him faithfully. What they heard him say and saw him do stayed with them. With one notable exception, they would soon take up the sower's sack and head into the fields as sowers themselves. They did this not simply because they admired Jesus so much, but because their lives had been transformed. The seed of God's Word had taken root in their hearts, and the produce is still bearing today!

110

This is where you and I come in. We are among those whose lives have been transformed in the grace of God through Christ. The seed of his Word has been broadcast in our lives. Yet in my own experience, I have to confess that the "soil" of my responsiveness is a bit of a mixed bag. There are plenty of hard-packed spaces where the Lord's Word just simply bounces off. Other parts of my life threaten the Word with the weeds of this world. I admit that sometimes I have promised the Lord more than I could deliver in terms of true discipleship, and there have been periods of burnout and lackluster devotion. Maybe you have had similar challenges on your spiritual journey.

Perhaps the parable isn't just about all those other people out there, as we sometimes think, all those other hardened souls who never give a thought to God, or those sporadic church-goers, or those easily dissuaded Christians. What if the parable is a mirror of our own openness to the Word of God -- or not?

2. RECEPTIVE SOIL

Here's something else to consider. Although Jesus the Sower broadcast his Word throughout the region, all around the countryside, going here and there to be sure as many people had the opportunity to respond as possible, still, he was very intentional about sharing the truths of the gospel with those who were most especially receptive. These were the ones he spent the most time with. It wasn't as if he cared nothing for others. Not at all. They were invited too. But there were these few, these strange fisherfolk, these people of the land with whom he walked day by day.

There is a principle espoused by leaders of the church growth movement of a generation or two ago that speaks to this matter of receptivity. The idea is to identify those people, those communities and regions where there is an evident responsiveness to the gospel, and concentrate evangelistic efforts there. Of course you can't know that in advance, though there are some conditions that promote receptivity. This means we have to sow the seed everywhere, and trust that God will show us where the harvest is truly ripening.

I expect this is not thought of often in our churches. We tend to keep on evangelizing those already committed, or so it seems. And we presume that the unchurched world is always unresponsive to the gospel. But clearly that is not so. There is widespread growth of the Christian movement today in many places heretofore regarded as "closed" to the gospel.

There is a sense in which the ordinary Christian is a sower of the gospel. In our daily lives, what we say, how we interact with others, what we stand for, we too are like the sower sent into the field. This is not our own choosing. It is because Christ has chosen us, warts and all, to walk each day with him.

TENANT TROUBLE

Listen to another parable. There was a landowner who planted a vineyard, put a fence around it, dug a wine press in it, and built a watchtower. Then he leased it to tenants and went to another country.
Matthew 21:33

Our Lord told some beautiful stories, heart gripping word-pictures that opened the shutters on the kingdom of heaven in our midst. We think of the Good Samaritan, or the Lost Sheep, or the Prodigal Son in this connection. Today's story is not one of those. He also spoke with amazing brevity about the kingdom, saying it's like a mustard seed, or treasure found in a field, or a pearl of great price. This story isn't like that. He told spiritually edifying parables, like the story of the Pharisee and publican in the temple, or the two builders whose homes were built on sand and rock. But the parable in today's Scripture reading isn't one of those, either. Jesus also told parables of judgment – the Great Banquet, the Wealthy Farmer, the Ten Bridesmaids -- and perhaps our parable today best fits into that category. I confess it's one of my least favorite parables – which puts me in the unpleasant company of the chief priests and Pharisees!

Twenty-six of the more than fifty parables of Jesus in the Gospels are taken directly from the ordinary life of folks who worked on farms and vineyards. New Testament scholars wrangle over whether today's story is a parable or an allegory. The difference may seem to be splitting hairs, but that's what scholars do! The Lord Jesus did not typically use allegory, so there are those who question the dominical origins of this story. Yet the parable appears in all three of the synoptic Gospels with slight variations, so that argument is difficult to sustain without damage to all the rest of the comments attributed to Christ. Those religious leaders who first heard this story had no doubt that it was a sharp criticism of their own husbandry of God's vineyard. The Bible says that they perceived these stories were about them, and they were enraged. At the very least, this story is about the abuse of trust. And in its severe presentation, it reveals the unprovoked wickedness that infects the human family.

Here, it seems to me, is part of the connection with our own lives today. Far too often we hear of human brutality – the merciless killing of a child by a parent or guardian, the terrorist bombing of a plaza filled with innocent bystanders, the senseless shooting in a school, restaurant, church or synagogue, and the list goes on. Whether we want to face it or not, there is a radical evil that resides inexplicably in the human psyche, cropping up in the everyday violence of our urban centers, the sudden deadly incident of road rage, and the international saber-rattling that seems intent on re-

113

starting the Cold War. It is this willful and unbridled evil that sticks out to me in Christ's story and brings it home to us.

There can be no good explanation for what the wicked tenants in Jesus' story did. The fact that the landowner had gone to a distant country seemed to be the only excuse they needed to do their worst. He had rented the vineyard to these people in good faith. In fact, he had gone beyond expectations by doing the planting, establishing a protective hedge, digging a wine press and erecting a warning tower. There really was nothing for the tenants to do except care for the growing crop, then harvest the fruit and pay the landowner the agreed portion. Then the landowner went away to a distant country.

Problems with absentee landlords are well documented. For many renters today, especially in dilapidated apartment buildings, the non-resident landlord comes across as uncaring, unresponsive to complaints, unapproachable. For too many landlords, being far from their property often means unpaid rents, trashing of the property, and also a general suspicion of the tenants. But this story is not about that.

For whatever reason – maybe it was greed, the desire to have it all for themselves; maybe it was a false sense of security, thinking that the landowner was so far away he could do nothing about the mistreatment of his servants; maybe it was envy, that the landowner was better off than they were; maybe it was fear, especially if they had not done a good job with the vineyard; or maybe it was just downright meanness – for whatever reason, the renters in Christ's story not only refused to pay the landowner what they owed, they abused his servants who came to collect it. Finally they killed his son for good measure!

But here the Lord Jesus paused to ask his hearers how they think the story should end. What will happen, do they think, when the landowner finally returns? And his hearers, evidently, had already caught the drift of the story. But they were painted into a corner. They couldn't very well suggest that these tenants would get away with it! Reason dictated that this vineyard owner would seek justice, even take the law into his own hands. He would put those wicked tenants to death, and then he would find others to care for the vineyard more responsibly. With a Scripture reference, Christ replied that in the same way the kingdom of God would be taken away from the unfaithful leadership of Israel and given to those who would produce good fruit. [Psalm 118:22-23] The implication was unmistakable, and the religious leaders in the group became intent on silencing Jesus by arresting him. But they were afraid to do so publicly because so many of the people held him in highest esteem, realizing he was a prophet.

So it's not a beautiful story, not one that touches the heart. It speaks, rather, of the undeniable reality of human sinfulness and affirms the conviction of divine judgment.

114

1. THE PROBLEM OF EVIL

It is interesting that Jesus Christ did not wrestle with what philosophers and theologians call "the problem of evil," that is, why there is evil in the world. He simply dealt with the reality of it. At the beginning of his ministry he encountered the full force of Satan's temptations and overcame them. But we're told that the Tempter departed, awaiting only an opportune time to return. [Luke 4:13] Jesus met people who were afflicted with what was thought of in that day as demon possession, and he cured them. He even dealt with the presence of evil within his own inner circle of friends. "Have I not called each of you, and one of you is a devil?" he once said, an obvious (to us) reference to the betrayal lurking in the shadows of the mind of Judas. [John 6:70] And to Peter he once said, "Get behind me, Satan... You are not on the side of God, but of men." [Matthew 16:23]

But the question of why bad things happen to people did come up in Christ's ministry. The general perspective at the time was that misfortune befalls those who have done something wrong. It was the same idea that the friends of Job had, but even though that biblical book showed the superficiality of that view, people still held it in the time of Christ. [Job 22:4-5] One day, when the disciples came upon a man who had been blind from birth, they asked the Lord: 'Who sinned, this man or his parents?' [John 9:2] But Christ made it clear that this condition was not the result of sin, either the man's own or his parents'. On another occasion, people were disturbed to hear that Governor Pilate had killed some Galileans and mingled their blood with their sacrifices. But Jesus told them those victims were not more sinful than others in Galilee, nor were the eighteen people who died when the tower of Siloam fell on them worse sinners than any others in Jerusalem. [Luke 13:1-4]

We do not suppose, in our day, that anyone who experiences calamity is being punished for wrongdoing. It's true that sometimes our misguided actions lead to disastrous consequences. But a person who is ill, beset with financial difficulties, or a victim of an accident is certainly no more of a sinner than others. Yet we continue to question why such tragedies occur.

A generation or more ago Rabbi Harold Kushner wrote a popular book with the title, *Why Bad Things Happen to Good People*. His adolescent son had died of a rare disease, and like any parent, he couldn't help asking how such a thing could happen to an innocent young boy. Many grapple with that kind of issue.

There are those, too, who think that all human wrongdoing is simply the result of Satanic influence. You may remember the TV comedian Flip Wilson who, years ago, jokingly excused his misbehavior saying, "The devil made me do it!" In this perspective, we human beings have no real responsibility for our actions. But the Bible doesn't see it that way. In Scripture, "the power of the devil... is never described as irresistible." (E. Brunner, *The Christian Doctrine of Creation and Redemption*, 138) The devil tempts, strives to lead us astray, but we have to allow ourselves to be so led. No one is excused. [Romans 2:1] The wicked tenants who brutalized the landowner's servants and killed his son did so of their own volition. No one, not even Satan, made them do it.

The story suggests a level of free moral agency for the tenants. They chose to do wrong, indeed they conspired together to do it. If God should intervene every time one of us commits a terrible act, there would be no human freedom, and thus no human responsibility to God or others. If we wonder why God doesn't stop the senseless brutality that flashes across the front page of the newspaper all too often, perhaps we could remember that God did not stop the horror of the Crucifixion of Christ. Yet the Cross itself became the instrument of divine redemption.

In the story Christ told, the tenants plotted and carried out murder, while the servants and the owner's son were the innocent victims of their heartlessness. Bad things happen. It's the way things are in this world which, as Scripture sees it, is estranged from God as a result of human rebellion and sin.

2. THE PROBLEM OF JUDGMENT

But the problem of evil isn't the only controversial issue in the parable Christ told. There is also the implication of divine judgment, which to many people today seems far too harsh for a loving God. The modern concept of God is embarrassed by this notion of divine judgment. Yet if there is no divine judgment beyond death, where is the justice for perpetrators of holocaust, genocide, mass murder? How does someone who bilks thousands of clients out of their life savings pay for something like that, or a child molester, or a terrorist? If there is no reckoning beyond the same fate of physical death we all must experience -- from Mother Teresa to the basest criminal -- then the whole concept of justice is at best temporal and transitory.

The overwhelming perspective of Scripture is that there is a divine reckoning for human misconduct. [Cf., Romans 2:3, Hebrews 9:27] But that recompense is not immediate. It is reserved for that day when God shall bring human history to a close. The biblical concept of divine judgment assures the reality of a level of justice that is not restricted to the fickle circumstances of courts and public opinion in this life but is wholly in the control of the One who knows and sees all.

Scripture makes it clear that all human beings are sinful. [Romans 3:23] Even those whose worst errors seem petty in comparison with the

116

most heinous actors in history must acknowledge that their life is spattered with the stains of sin. None of us is righteous, says Scripture, not a single one. [Psalm 14:3, Romans 3:10]

This is not the only parable in which Jesus called attention to divine judgment. We hear it in the story of Lazarus and the rich man, one in heaven and the other not. [Luke 16:19-31] And in the illustration of those who either did or did not minister to the least of these as to Christ himself. [Matthew 25:31-36] And in the parable of the talents, where one who had been entrusted with a little did nothing with what he did have, and thus lost everything. [Matthew 25:14-30] Jesus felt it necessary to warn his followers of the dangers of willful disobedience of divine expectations. It's a warning our own generation should heed.

3. THE PROBLEMS RESOLVED

Because of human frailty and sin, our prospects in the face of such a Judgment Day are dire. Except for this. The one who finds forgiveness and new life in Christ has no need to fear this judgment. Rather, on that Day the believer enters the eternal joy of the Presence of the Lord. 'Though our sins be as scarlet, they shall be as white as snow.' [Isaiah 1:18] What God sees in the one who trusts in Christ is not our wrongdoing, which would condemn us, but rather Christ's righteousness, which saves us.

This is a way of understanding the cryptic comment that the kingdom will be taken away from those who think they deserve it and given to those who realize they really don't! It is only in Christ that the problem of evil, and our share in it, is overcome. He is the divine intervention that answers the injustice of unprovoked, unmitigated evil. His atoning death offers life to all who will trust in him, life beyond this life, mercy in the face of divine judgment.

A PLACE OF HONOR

When he noticed how the guests chose the places of honor, he told them a parable. Luke 14:7

The Lord Jesus was keenly sensitive to the brokenness in our world. So often this was evident in his response to the pains and illnesses of the people he encountered. We look in on Luke's report today as Jesus was on his way to a dinner engagement one sabbath at the home of a notable Pharisee. By the way, for folks who couldn't get along with Jesus, the Pharisees tended to spend a lot of time with him! Luke tells us there was a man "in front of him" who was suffering from dropsy, a condition of swelling which greatly affected one's mobility. Jesus realized, of course, that the religious leaders of the town would be watching his every move, so he first asked them if it was lawful to cure people on the sabbath or not. He knew what they were thinking, since he not only was sensitive to the physical illness of the unfortunate man, but also to the spiritual brokenness of those daring him to make a mistake. To their credit, they didn't say anything. If they had held to the position that such a humanitarian gift would be a transgression of sabbath rules, they would have invited the charge of callous indifference to the plight of a fellow human being. When they were silent, Jesus "took him and healed him, and sent him away." [Luke 14:4] Then he asked the bystanders if any one of them had a child or an ox who fell into a well, wouldn't they immediately pull it out, even it happened on a sabbath day? They had no reply for that, either.

Then when the Lord arrived at the house of the Pharisee and people were gathering around the table for the meal, he noticed that the guests were trying to get as close to their host as possible, the places of honor. It was a matter of prestige to be closely associated with the successful Pharisee. Pride, envy, jealousy, anger, hurt feelings all swirled around the atmosphere, evidence of the brokenness in our world. And Doctor Luke says that when Jesus noticed their attitudes and actions, he told them a parable.

1. A STORY WITH TWO LEVELS

A parable is a story with two levels. It typically describes a hypothetical occurrence from everyday life that any listener could relate to – level one -- but invariably it points to a deeper spiritual truth – level two. Bible scholars debate whether or not today's passage is really a parable. But Luke called it a parable, and he ought to know, since he alone records some of the Lord's most poignant parables. Admittedly, this one is not in the form of a story, but rather a scene that would have been familiar to his hearers, a wedding feast. A wedding in those days, as is often the case today, was a social occasion. And today it's not unusual for the bridal party and invited guests to enjoy a banquet. The hosts of the party go to great lengths to make sure the event goes well, even using place cards at the table so folks know where to sit. In the situation Jesus described, though, there were no place names. Jesus seems to be suggesting that etiquette would demand that one not seek the place of honor, lest the host come along and nudge you aside for someone of higher standing! Instead, find a lower place at the table, and then maybe the host will notice and move you up in the sight of all.

Hold on a second! Why would the Lord Jesus, affirmed in the New Testament as the Word of God made flesh without whom nothing was made, and who came into the world to defeat the powers of evil, sin and death – why would Jesus trouble himself about the trifling issue of where people sit at the table? What about the really big sins of the world like mass murder, terrorism, unprovoked war, human trafficking and so on? Wouldn't it be better to tell a story addressing these major concerns? Evidently the table etiquette is just level one of the scene, though. Something else is going on here, too. The scene concludes with one of the Lord's favorite sentiments: 'For all who exalt themselves will be humbled, and those who humble themselves will be exalted.' [Cf., Matthew 23:12] We – and no doubt those first hearers – realize Jesus isn't talking about table manners at all.

He's addressing the brokenness in us and around us. The perfectly normal desire to be recognized, to put ourselves forward, to get the best seats, can easily digress into a complete preoccupation with self. And that is usually at the heart of all the sinfulness we can think of. When our desires, ambitions and perceived needs become all-consuming, and when we obsess over feelings of frustration and rage due to some slight or mistreatment, there is practically no limit to the rationalization we can manufacture to excuse whatever we want to do to get even or get ahead. From these seemingly insignificant personal issues the seeds of far greater ills are sown. That's level two of the illustration, a sort of egocentric idolatry. Is it a coincidence that Jesus spoke to this issue in a gathering of Pharisees?

2. THE CHALLENGE OF HUMILITY

Yet when the Lord advises his followers to practice humility, that does not sit well with our own me-first generation. We suspect it rang hollow in the ears of Christ's first listeners, too. If this were the only instance of Jesus' comments like this we might be able to downplay his emphasis on humility. But that isn't the case. There are those sayings that declare the last shall be first and the first last, for instance. [Cf., Luke 13:30; Matthew 20:16] And the teaching about the necessity of becoming like children to enter the kingdom of heaven. [Matthew 18:3] And Jesus' own description of himself as 'meek and lowly,' or 'gentle and humble in heart.' [Matthew 11:28] Humility was to be a trait of Christ's followers. There's no getting around it.

We should be cautious in our thinking about this, because there is such a thing as false humility. We sometimes fish for compliments in this way, don't we? I'm reminded of that humorous song by Mac Davis years ago: "O Lord, it's hard to be humble, when you're perfect in every way!" As soon as we think we're pretty humble, we've lost it! There is also an unhealthy self-abasement that can lead to many other problems. An inferiority complex or self-hatred is essentially just an inverted pride. That's not what Christ was talking about, either. The humility he expects of his own people is the unequivocal acknowledgment that God alone is God, and not we ourselves. [Psalm 100:3] In the words of the apostle Paul, we are not to think more highly of ourselves than we ought to think. [Romans 12:3] There is a healthy self-esteem, in other words, but it can get overbalanced if we aren't careful. C.S. Lewis said humility is not thinking less of ourselves, but thinking of ourselves less!

The Lord urges us, with the help of the Holy Spirit, to reign in our natural impulse to think first, or even only of ourselves. How counter-cultural this is! Our society is built on personal advancement, acquisition of material things that testify to our worth and success. Humility is scorned as weakness. So Christ's counsel to select the lowest place at the table grates on our nerves.

The Lord's closest friends struggled with it, too. The disciples seemed to be perpetually arguing about which of them was the greatest. [Cf., Mark 9:34] The brothers James and John took the matter to the extreme, requesting positions of high authority and privilege in Christ's kingdom. [Mark 10:37] When the other disciples heard it, they weren't happy. They, too, harbored some personal ambitions, no doubt! Yet often Jesus told them that he came to serve, not to be served, and that they too must cultivate the attitude of servanthood. [Matthew 20:26-28] There was no position more humble in that society than the servant. So this level of concern for others, this capacity to put the needs of others before our own, is a mark of Christian discipleship. It wasn't easy for the original Twelve disciples, and it isn't easy for us.

There is scarcely a Christian virtue more fitting for our consideration in the season of Lent than humility. It arises not from feelings of inferiority, but from an acute awareness of our sinfulness and need of a Savior! The words of the Psalmist echo down the halls of this season: "Have mercy on me, O God, according to your steadfast love... For I

120

know my transgressions, and my sin is ever before me... Against you, you alone have I sinned, and done what is evil in your sight... Create in me a clean heart, O God, and put a new and right spirit within me." [Psalm 51: 1, 3, 4,10] Christian humility is based in a sense of our unworthiness before God which leads to repentance, and at the same time it reflects our gratitude that divine grace revealed in Christ forgives and restores us to life with God.

3. MODELED AFTER CHRIST

The humility to which we are called is also modeled after the humility Christ exhibited in his own life. As the Letter to the Philippians has it, 'though he was in the form of God, he did not regard equality with God as something to be exploited, but emptied himself and became obedient to the point of death on a cross.' [Philippians 2:6ff] His humility was revealed in his total commitment to the will of the heavenly Father, and that was itself a source of unmatched power. Christian humility is not the "doormat" mentality we often think it is. It is the surrender of our prideful will to the gracious will of God that stands against the evils of this world and in ourselves.

If we realize that we don't deserve a place of honor before God, if we are so grateful for God's amazing kindness in inviting us to the banquet that we seek only the lowest place, then we are wonderfully surprised to be granted a place of honor anyway! That's what happened in the scenario Jesus gave. The humble guest, having chosen a lower position, was noticed by the host and brought forward in the presence of all. This is grace!

121

A STUDY IN CONTRAST

Two men went up to the temple to pray, one a Pharisee and the other a tax collector. Luke 18:10

Watching the coverage of Pope Francis' visit to Washington DC this past week underscored for me the impact that a spiritual leader can have, even in our largely secular society. Much of the attention was due to his position as the titular head of more than a billion Catholics worldwide -- about 17% of the total population – and Pontiffs like the long-tenured John Paul II also drew large crowds. But perhaps it is even more the case that Francis' evident popularity is the public perception that he has the common touch. In his welcoming remarks President Obama noted the Pope's 'unique qualities as a person,' his humility as well as his compassion and love for the marginalized. In this, the President observed, Francis is for many a 'living example of Jesus' teachings.' Even some 76% of Protestants, we are told, have a positive attitude toward the Pope. Whether or not we are "Francis Fans," it is hard to think of another religious leader in our time who has generated such enthusiasm wherever he goes. Perhaps the closest to this phenomenon in Protestant circles were the huge crowds associated with Billy Graham Crusades in the mid-years of the 20th century. More recently and from another faith tradition altogether, the Dali Lama seems to be well-received in his travels, though not with the out-pouring of affection seen in the Pope's visits around the world.

Humility and celebrity are not mutually exclusive, but it's not an easy combination! To have the world's acclaim is pretty heady stuff, I would imagine. Movie stars, sports figures, musicians, government leaders live in a fish bowl. Quite a number of them flame out under the pressure. So it is gratifying to notice that a person like Pope Francis can smoothly convey strength and meekness, wisdom and humor, kindness and principle, humility in the glare of celebrity.

Those were surely some of the traits that attracted large gatherings to Jesus Christ. That popularity, too, was a source of great frustration for his antagonists. Among the latter were those who are described in our Scripture reading this morning as being 'confident in their own righteousness, looking down on everyone else.' [Luke 18:9 NIV] To these folks Christ told the story we know as the Parable of the Pharisee and the Tax Collector.

The word "parable" means to cast alongside, that is, to draw a comparison, to show a contrast. While it often reflects something of human nature, the parable typically illumines the divine nature as well. This parable of the two men who went to the temple to pray is certainly a study in contrast.

In those days the Jerusalem temple was a very busy place. There were morning and evening sacrifices, and other services in between. At special times during the year the temple was the scene of dramatic worship services that drew thousands of visitors. In the time of Christ these activities were going on in the midst of a massive construction project, as King Herod sought to endear himself to the people (and feather his own cap) by enlarging the temple. His ploy didn't really work in terms of gaining the respect of the populace, but there is no doubt that everyone was impressed by the huge building program, including the disciples of Jesus. The temple was the ritualistic heart of Jewish religious life in those days. But it was the synagogue, rather than the temple, that was the place for religious instruction. The temple on Mount Zion in Jerusalem contained not only the Court of the Gentiles, the Court of Women, the Court of Israel and the Holy of Holies, but also in the anterooms encircling the temple itself there were seven synagogues. Here preaching and teaching services were held daily. It was probably in one of the synagogues that Mary and Joseph located the twelve-year-old Jesus after they had missed him when they started out for Nazareth following a religious festival in Jerusalem. [Luke 2:46]

So the setting of this parable was a busy place. We are not given details of the service these two men attended, nor where exactly they were in the temple. Some scholars believe it may have been during the afternoon sacrifice, and that in fact the two featured in the story would have been among many other worshipers gathered there. There were no pews or seats of any kind in the temple, so during prayers, some would stand, some would kneel, some would bow, some would look heavenward. But it's as if Jesus purposely portrays a scene where these two fellows seem to be the only ones in the temple at this time. All attention is turned to them.

Jesus describes one of the men as a Pharisee and the other as a tax collector. You could scarcely have imagined two more different people in that day. A study in contrast. Let's notice a few of these differences.

1. THE PHARISEE

The first man is introduced simply as a Pharisee. This immediately raises a red flag for those of us who have spent time in the Gospels. We remember that Jesus frequently had run-ins with these folks, calling them 'whitened sepulchers' and 'hypocrites.' [Matthew 23:27] He warned his followers to beware of the 'leaven of the Pharisees,' that is, their insidious capacity to do evil while appearing to do good. [Matthew 16:6] Our image of them, drawn mostly from the Gospels and even this parable, is not very favorable. And we can't forget that they made unprecedented alliances with their rivals the Sadducees and the despised Roman authorities, leading to Christ's betrayal, trial and execution.

But perhaps we can suspend our preconceptions long enough to recognize that in Palestine the Pharisees were often highly esteemed. The Sadducees, comprised of the priestly caste, were associated with the temple and its practices. But the Pharisees were far more closely aligned with the synagogues. They were people of prayer who pored over the ancient scriptures and commentaries, tithed faithfully, and were quite strict in their interpretations of the moral code. The Pharisees were laymen, not religious professionals. There were never more than about 3,000 Pharisees at any one time, yet they had major influence despite their relatively small number. They shared seats on the Sanhedrin -- the Supreme Court of the day -- with the Sadducee party.

To the people who first heard Christ's parable, the Pharisee was a man of solid reputation, an upstanding citizen, a deeply religious person, a leader in the community. The Pharisee was well regarded, well educated, and often well heeled! The apostle Paul, you may remember, was a Pharisee before becoming a follower of Christ. [Philippians 3:5] Nicodemus, the man who approached Jesus by night, was a Pharisee. It was he who went with Joseph of Arimathea to remove the body of Christ from the cross. [John 3:1; John 19:39] So they weren't all hypocrites, and they weren't all intent on doing Christ harm. But Jesus was hard on this group because there were indeed so many who had the tendency to be self-righteous. That questionable trait characterized the man in the Lord's parable.

We are given a clue that the story won't go well for him when Jesus says, 'He stood and prayed with himself.' [RSV] Does this mean he stood off by himself to pray, as the NIV translation suggests? Or does it indicate, as some translators have rendered it, that he was praying about himself, or even to himself? We can't help noticing that there are a lot of "I's" in his prayer: 'I thank you that I am not as other men... I fast twice a week, I tithe of all I get, I'm not a sinner like this other fellow, this tax collector.'

2. THE TAX COLLECTOR

That brings us, then, to the second man in the story, the tax collector. Again we have some preconceived ideas about him based on other accounts from scripture. We know, for instance, that a tax collector in that society was despised by the community because, as an Israelite, he was considered to be a collaborator with the Roman occupiers. The Romans required taxes of all subjects, of course, and they set a certain rate. But it was up to the local publicans to collect that tribute, plus any amount they felt they could get away with to line their own pockets.

124

The tax collector also worked in direct competition to the temple tax system. A faithful Hebrew head of household was required to pay a tithe of ten percent to the temple, and there were other offerings as well. But the Roman taxes were levied over and above the accustomed temple tax and without regard to it. Little wonder that it was said that an ordinary person would likely cross the street to the other side if he saw a tax collector coming his way. You remember that Zacchaeus was a tax collector. [Luke 19:2] He may have been in that sycamore tree as much because no one else wanted to stand near him as to see over the crowd! Another well-known tax collector was Matthew, or Levi, whom Jesus called to be one of the original twelve disciples. [Matthew 9:9]

Mention the phrase 'tax collector' in first century Jerusalem, though, and someone in the group would probably have spat on the ground! They were generally regarded as cheats, scoundrels, turncoats, profiteers, you name it.

This man in Jesus' story couldn't have been more different from the Pharisee. And his prayer couldn't have been more different, either. Jesus describes him as 'standing afar off,' standing at a distance. We don't know where the Pharisee stood to pray, but we expect it was in a prominent place in the temple. But this tax collector stood in the shadows, shrank back away from the crowd, sought not to be noticed. Instead of lifting his eyes to heaven, he was bent over, and he beat his own breast in an act of contrition as he prayed, 'God, have mercy on me a sinner!'

Was this man a tither as the Pharisee was? We don't know. Maybe. Or maybe not. Was he as free of moral wrongdoing as the Pharisee. Evidently not, because he was so conscious of his own sin. Did he regard himself as superior to any of his neighbors? On the contrary, he thought he didn't deserve even to stand with them.

No, a greater contrast between two individuals in worship could hardly be drawn in so few words. They were polar opposites.

3. SURPRISE

Now the surprise comes at the end of the story. Of course we aren't surprised by the surprise any more, because we've heard the story so many times. But those who first heard it, you can be sure, were surprised. When that publican prayed, 'God, have mercy on me a sinner,' there might have been people in the crowd around Jesus who broke out laughing! 'Whoo boy! That's a good one.' They would have thought the story was over, the joke was finished. There's no way on earth that this evil character could have God's mercy. There's zero possibility that he would be able to find a way into God's good graces after all he's done. Especially in comparison with that fine Pharisee over there. The Pharisee was a fellow you'd invite home to dinner, hope to go into business with. But this tax collector? Expecting some sort of merciful response from a holy God? Impossible!

But before the giggles die down, Jesus turns things upside down. He said the tax collector went to his home justified rather than the Pharisee.

For this, no one was prepared. The laughter stopped. The disciples looked puzzled. The scribes and Pharisees looked angry. Those in the crowd who were skeptical of Jesus became even more so. This wasn't turning out the way it was supposed to. In conclusion Jesus said, 'Everyone who exalts himself will be humbled, and he who humbles himself will be exalted.'

That's the heart of the matter. The Pharisee had exalted himself; the tax collector had humbled himself. In conventional morality there was no comparison between them. The Pharisee had that hands down. But the salvation that Christ brings is not based on good works, not based even on our morality. The justification available in Jesus Christ is the free grace of Almighty God that forgives sins and makes us fit for life with God. What is required of us is our recognition of our sinfulness, our need of a Savior, and the humble acceptance of God's offer of grace.

Once that grace is received, then we can talk again about righteous living, but first things first. Let's not be praying with ourselves in haughty awareness of all we've done for God. Rather, let's consider our unworthiness in the light of Christ's matchless love, and receive that grace with thanksgiving.

The Pharisee prayed as if he needed no forgiveness, and he got none. The publican prayed for forgiveness, and received it! The Pharisee sought to justify himself before God, but he was not justified. The tax collector knew he had no standing of his own before God, but in his humility and trust in God's mercy, he went home justified. To be justified means to be "right-wised."

God's holiness cannot countenance sin, whether the sin of arrogance and self-righteousness as with the Pharisee, or the sin of greed and immorality which plagued the tax collector. God will not overlook sin. Further, the human condition of sinfulness and rebellion is just as true of the seemingly righteous person as it is of the obviously wicked one. And we are powerless to change that! Yet God's redemptive purpose is not thwarted even by our sin, for he has sent his Son to make atonement for all who believe. When we look to Jesus for mercy and forgiveness, God counts that act of trust and surrender as the righteousness of Christ. Through the sacrifice of Christ, we are made whole in the sight of God.

The story makes it clear that Jesus is closer to one sinner who repents than to a hundred so-called righteous people who think they have no need to repent. [Luke 15:7] Genuine humility before God is no pathological self-deprecation, no 'poor self-esteem.' It is simply the

126

acknowledgment that we have no hope of salvation apart from Jesus Christ. Yet in him we are lifted up from the hopelessness that our own willfulness condemns us to. We are made joint heirs with Christ in his kingdom.

But let's be careful. Because we may find ourselves leaving this parable saying something like, 'Lord, I thank thee that I'm not like that old Pharisee was!'

APRIL FOOL

Then he told them a parable: "The land of a rich man produced abundantly." Luke 12:16

Did anyone prank you for April Fool's Day this past Friday? Or perhaps you playfully tricked someone else! I was fortunate enough to escape the mischief again this year. But I did wonder where the custom came from. The origins of the quirky observance are not fully known, but some maintain it stems from the 1500s when France adopted the Gregorian calendar in place of the Julian one. This meant the first day of the new year would be January 1 instead of April 1. Those who failed to get the memo, continuing to celebrate New Year's in April, were branded as April Fools. There are other evidences of an observance in antiquity, but it's, uh, foolish to try to sort them out.

We all know what it's like to feel foolish, especially when we've made a gaffe that embarrasses us. Most often we just laugh at ourselves, but sometimes the consequences of our mistake can be more serious. I saw a bumper sticker the other day that read: "Caution: I do dumb stuff!" That warning might be plastered on the billboard of the human condition. We all do and say things we later regret or regard as foolish. To fall victim to our own naivete or ignorance feels worse than being harmlessly tricked by someone else. On the other hand, to be maliciously duped by another, particularly in this day of cyber-fraud, is not a laughing matter. We remember some proverbial thoughts along this line: 'A fool and his money are soon parted,' and, 'It is better to keep one's mouth shut and be thought a fool than to open it and remove all doubt!'

Webster's dictionary describes a fool as a person lacking in judgment or prudence. It also mentions that in royal households of the past there were court jesters who played the fool as a source of comic relief. Our thinking about foolhardiness today is not just due to the recent first day of April, nor even about two multimillionaires making fools of themselves at the Academy Awards, but more precisely because the parable from the Gospel of Luke that is our focus uses the word "fool" quite dramatically. In fact the story is sometimes referred to as the Parable of the Rich Fool.

1. THE PRESENTING PROBLEM

Before we get into it, though, we should note the "presenting problem" that was the occasion for the story. Almost always in Luke our Lord's parables were responses to specific situations. In this instance "someone in the crowd" listening to Christ's teachings got the Lord's attention and made a unique request. He wanted Jesus, acknowledged by now as a spiritual teacher and healer, to persuade his brother to divide the family inheritance. Evidently the patriarch of the family has died and the executor of the estate is the older son. But, in the opinion of this younger sibling, his brother has been intentionally dragging his feet in parceling out the deceased parent's property. So he wants Jesus to persuade the guy to get it done. He makes it sound like a matter of justice. 'It's what is due me,' he seems to say. But the issue isn't really justice, and Jesus sees through him. It's his impatience for the money, his greed, in other words. The Lord deflects the petition by pointing out that he held no elected position that would allow him to arbitrate the situation. 'Who made me a judge over you?' he asked. In fact, as we know, Jesus did have such authority, though he chose not to exercise it in that way. The man had no answer, perhaps because he realized he had overstepped.

You may have noticed that there are only two occasions in the Gospel of Luke when the Lord Jesus was asked to rebuke or correct a third party. The other incident was the familiar account of Martha asking Jesus to tell her sister Mary to get busy helping out in the kitchen! [Luke 10:38-42] In that exchange, as in the one we're considering today, Jesus actually rebuked the one making the request! 'Be on your guard against all kinds of greed,' said Jesus to this man and to the gathered crowd. And that comment led to this parable that appears only in Luke.

2. A GOOD PROBLEM TO HAVE

On the surface of it, the chief character in the story was dealing with a good problem to have. Almost anyone listening to Jesus that day would have been a bit envious of the fellow. He had a successful agribusiness even before the bumper crops came in. Jesus described him as a "rich" man. Then the abundance of harvest created the problem of what to do with all the excess. His barns weren't big enough to store it all. So he decided to tear down the inadequate barns and build new, larger ones to provide space for the grain. Thinking this would solve his problem, he started daydreaming about the future. He pictured himself with a lifetime of ease, no worries, not a care in the world. But he hadn't taken into consideration the fact that his life was subject to immediate and drastic change. "You fool!" God said. That very night would be his last, and then who would benefit from all his wealth?

This is a disquieting story on several fronts. It underscores how transitory and uncertain life is, just in case we have overlooked that fact – as did that farmer. And it points out that this world's material goods, important as they are, cannot be our ultimate value system. They, too, one day will be gone, or at least unavailable to us. In a comment that reminds us of the Sermon on the Mount, the Lord Jesus ended this story with the warning that to store up earthly treasures can do no good if we are not interested in our relationship to God, treasures in heaven, as it were. [Matthew 6:20] Jesus, here and elsewhere, expected his followers to put their trust in God, not in personal wealth or individual achievement. Christ challenged the accepted standards of success for that day and for our own. What made the man a fool was not his business acumen, not even his decision to build bigger barns, but the self-deception that he had everything under control, that nothing could go wrong. He was living as if there would be no accountability for his actions, and as if the future was in his own hands.

3. 'FOOL' BOTHERS US

It's this word 'fool' that bothers us the most. I can hardly read this parable without remembering with a smile the character Mr T played in that old TV show "The A Team." If you recall, he did not suffer fools gladly! "Fool!" he would cry, when someone disappointed him. The Bible has quite a bit to say about human foolishness. The wisdom literature of the Bible contrasts those who are foolish in their rebelliousness against God with those who are wise, seeking after God. The Book of Proverbs suggests that human foolishness is the inclination to trust our own hearts, our own way of thinking, our own way of doing things, rather than to seek the wisdom that God provides. [Cf., Proverbs 28:26] It thinks of wickedness as a kind of wrong-headedness, without regard for the needs of others or the clear will of God. Ecclesiastes declares that 'wisdom excels folly as light excels darkness. The wise have eyes to see, but fools walk in darkness.' [Ecclesiastes 2:13-14] In Jesus' parable there was no sense of responsibility for the farmer's neighbors or his community. His attention was riveted on what made him feel personally successful and secure.

The Psalms see human folly as rejection of God. We think of those verses that read, 'The fool says in his heart, "There is no God."' [Psalm 14:1; 53:1] We make a mistake, though, when we limit this perspective to professed atheists. There probably were very few avowed atheists in ancient Israel, unlike in our own time and culture. Today there are even commercials on TV advocating atheism. I have known several atheists over the years, and I would describe none of them as fools. I have thought of them as misguided, hoping they would have a change of heart. Personally, I am reluctant to refer to anyone as a fool, remembering our Lord's dire statement about that. [Cf., Matthew 5:22] But really I have more trouble with folks who are, for lack of a better term, "practicing atheists." By this I mean that there are many people who would claim some sort of belief in God, but who actually live <u>as if</u> there is no God, and especially as if there is

130

no accountability to God for their attitudes and actions. They couldn't be bothered to think about what God's will might be in this situation or that. Like the man in the parable, they are in their own world, literally.

It is this self-centeredness that is the source of greed. And that abiding covetousness distances us from God. The man who came to Jesus hoping to enlist his aid in getting what he wanted from his brother was absorbed in his own desires and dreams. He could certainly put that money to good use! But that attitude had cost him more than he realized. Instead of a brother he had a rival. Instead of following Jesus as a disciple, he came recruiting Jesus for his own purposes.

4. GRACE IN THE WARNING

When we recount the parables of the Good Shepherd or the Prodigal Son or the Good Samaritan, we are grateful for the radiance of divine grace they provide. But what about this story? Where is the gospel in the parable of the Rich Fool? It is found in Christ's admonition to be more concerned about our spiritual treasure than the material possessions that we typically work so hard for. There is grace in the divine welcome of the parables, yes, but there is grace also in the divine warning we find in them. We might think of it a bit like the weather reports we're so familiar with. We rely on the day-by-day weather forecasts to plan activities. But when the storm warning interrupts our "regularly scheduled programming," we may be disgruntled. There is no doubt, though, that these alerts can save lives. This parable of the man whose priorities were skewed to the point of having no consideration for anyone or anything besides himself is like a storm alert. It may make us uncomfortable but it reminds us of what is most important, and could save us from the foolishness of self-centeredness, and thinking that we can manage on our own without God.

Maybe this parable is especially fitting in the season of Lent. This is the season when we ask ourselves if there is an adjustment we need to make in terms of our spiritual health. Do we need to reconsider our own blessings, think about our own priorities, and contemplate afresh our Savior's call to store up heavenly treasure? The man in the story talked to himself, saying 'Soul, relax! You've got it made.' Sometimes we need an inner talking-to, but the message would be different. 'Soul, remember that you are a child of God, bought with the price of the Cross. Don't be foolish enough to let other things get in the way of being the person God calls you to be.'

131

DRESSED DOWN

Once more Jesus spoke to them in parables, saying: 'The kingdom of heaven may be compared to a king who gave a wedding banquet for his son. Matthew 22:1-2

It may seem a bit out of sync to talk about the parables of Jesus at a time when we are still reeling from the effects of wild fires, the massacre in Las Vegas, and the devastating hurricanes. People outside the church think we believers are out of touch, old fashioned, mired in the ancient biblical stories when the 21st century scarcely will let us catch our breath from one tragedy, scandal or international threat to another. But to us, the words of that old hymn still resonate: "Tell me the stories of Jesus I love to hear; Things I would ask him to tell me If he were here." [W.H. Parker]

But not all the stories of Jesus are so easy for us to hear, and we are sure they weren't very well received among his first listeners, either. The suggested lectionary readings in recent weeks have presented us with some pretty challenging parables as we make our way through the Gospel of Matthew this year. There was, for example, the story of a man whose two sons were asked to work in the family vineyard, but the first refused to do so and the second agreed to go. But the story went on to say that the youth who first refused, decided to go to work after all, while the young man who initially said he would go didn't make it. [Matthew 21:28-31] Then there was the parable of another householder who rented his vineyard to people who proved to be wicked, not only refusing to pay their rent, but abusing the owner's servants who came to collect and then ultimately killing the man's son in a vain attempt to gain his inheritance for themselves. [Matthew 21:33-41] These stories, and the two under consideration today, we realize are parables of God's dealings with humanity, of divine opportunity and human obstinacy. They aren't the beautiful, heart-touching stories Jesus told – like the Good Samaritan, or the Lost Sheep, or the Prodigal Son. And they aren't like the one-liners of the kingdom of heaven, such as the mustard seed, or the pearl of great price, or the hidden treasure found in a field. They aren't even like the spiritually edifying parables of the Pharisee and the publican, or the new wine in old wine skins. Today's stories belong in a different category. They are stories of divine judgment, like the separation of sheep from goats at the Great Banquet or the Ten Bridesmaids, five of whom failed to prepare adequately for the feast. Our Scripture lesson today presents two stories about human willfulness in the face of God's gracious welcome.

The first parable, the parable of the Wedding Feast for the King's Son, is similar to the story in the Gospel of Luke about a man who gave a

132

feast and invited many guests, but when the appointed day arrived, they all sent their last-minute excuses. Infuriated, the host sent out the servant into the community to bring in "the poor, the maimed and the blind," all the less fortunate folks who would usually not be included in such a social occasion. The first invitees were then purposefully excluded. [Luke 14:15-24] Matthew's account of the parable bears similarity also to the story of the vineyard owner and the wicked tenants mentioned a moment ago. The second story in our text, though, the one about inappropriate wedding attire, is found only in Matthew. While it is linked to the first parable, its message is a bit different.

Let me invite you to address with me the question of how these parables from antiquity have any relevance to our modern life. A simple train of thought might focus matters for us: Revelation, Repudiation, and Restoration.

1. REVELATION

The wedding day has arrived, as the story opens, and the king sends his emissaries to let the invited guests know that everything is ready for his son's feast. It's time to come! We are given to understand that the wedding invitations had been sent out at an earlier time, and thus the people of the community had plenty of opportunity to arrange their schedules. If someone unfortunately could not go, he or she would make sure to send regrets early enough so the king could plan accordingly. But it was no small thing to be invited to the king's palace! So it's very likely that everybody would have wanted to attend the feast to honor the young prince and his new bride. Even if someone really didn't want to go, it probably was in his or her best interest to attend anyway! The invitation went out.

This is where we need to skip to the end of our reading for today where the Lord notes that many are called but few are chosen. [verse 14] On first blush the comment doesn't quite seem to fit the context. But if we think of the invitation as God's call, a call that has been extended from the time of the Garden of Eden to the present, it begins to take on a different feel.

Think of this invitation, this call, as God's revelation to humankind. It's an invitation that has come to everyone. But someone will say, 'I haven't received any divine invitation! People talk about being called, and receiving an invitation from God, but I assure you, nothing like that has ever happened to me.' Well, maybe not in so many words, but look at it this way. Each of us was born, we've been given life on this earth. That's an invitation in itself, an invitation to consider that there is a Source for our life, a Creator behind our own existence, and the world we live in. There is not a single person alive who hasn't received this invitation to believe in the

133

God who made him or her. But it's true that there are folks who do not accept the invitation to be in relationship with God simply because they exist. So God has provided additional invitations. The wonders of nature, for instance, can be an invitation to us to acknowledge the Creator behind it all. The Bible tells us that the firmament and the stars above testify of God's creative power. [e.g., Psalm 19:1] It's part of God's invitation to humanity.

But of course there are folks who see the same natural world we do and perceive no notion of a divine invitation. For them the world is a purely mechanistic reality, moving according to predetermined laws with no purposeful beginning or end, and indeed no real meaning apart from what one may contrive on his or her own. It's an invitation, a revelation, but not one everyone will accept it as such.

So there have been other invitations, too. In addition to our own existence and the natural world -- what might be thought of as general revelation -- there is the special revelation of God to people. In this case God directly interacts with people, speaking to them, making covenant with them, warning them. And the record of these interactions has been preserved in yet another form of invitation, the Holy Scriptures. In the Bible we have the story of God's engraved invitation to people to be in loving and faithful relationship to our Creator. Scripture makes it clear that even these repeated invitations have not always been accepted. Despite God's gracious gifts of covenant and law and prophet, often the invitations have gone unheeded.

Still, this has not yet exhausted the invitation God has offered to the world, the self-revelation of the Almighty. No, there has been yet one more supreme invitation: God's ultimate self-revelation in the Person and work of Jesus Christ, God's Son. But it is true that not everyone receives that invitation cordially, either. In fact, just as in Christ's parable of the tenants in the vineyard, the Son of God was actually put to death. [Matthew 21:33ff] Yet the divine revelation wasn't over! Christ arose, ascended into heaven to await the day of his return in glory, and through his Spirit he empowers and sustains his church to the present hour! Through the faithful witness of the church God's invitation continues to go out.

You would think, then, that with these multiple invitations, everyone in the world would be eager to come to the Sovereign Lord's banquet.

2. REPUDIATION

But we know better. As in the parable Christ told, people have their excuses for not responding to the call and invitation of God. To them the reasons are justifiable. Luke's version of the story has guests asking to be excused from attending the feast due to urgent business matters: the purchase of a field, or a new yoke of oxen. [Luke 14:16ff] One was just recently married and so couldn't be expected to attend. These reasons for inattendance strike us as superficial. Wouldn't that new field be there tomorrow, and the difference of one more day would make little difference in the training of those oxen. And surely the newlyweds would be welcome at the king's feast, and their honeymoon would be far more luxurious as a result. Now in Matthew's version of the story there is no attempt to make excuses. The invited guests, once notified that the feast was ready, simply would not come! When word came back to the king of this non-response, he sent more servants out to alert the people that all was ready, no doubt thinking there must have been some misunderstanding. But this time the servants were appalled when the invitees made fun of the king and his son, even went so far as to murder the king's emissaries.

There is an unmistakable rebelliousness in the attitude of those first guests, a repudiation of the king's gracious invitation. They not only refuse to come to the palace for the feast, they pretend the king has no authority of them, that they can do as they please without fear of reprisal.

This seems hard for us to understand. What would motivate the king's subjects to take such an attitude? We could speculate that they were unwilling subjects of this king, that perhaps they lived in a conquered land and felt no allegiance to this sovereign. But the story doesn't say that. Or we might suggest that these initially invited guests repudiated the king's invitation as a first step toward insurrection and rebellion, perhaps the overthrow of the government and the establishment of a new king. Such things did happen in that day. But the story doesn't say that, either. There really is no clue in the story as to why these people behaved so rudely and cruelly. But we remind ourselves that the Storyteller has a particular perspective on the world of human affairs. It is a divine perspective. He sees the behavior as willful disobedience and rebellion against the God of the universe.

Now this is where the parable takes a turn toward divine judgment. The king sends his troops to destroy the city and commands that his servants go into the countryside, along the main highway, and bring in as many people as they find, the good and the bad, to eat the wedding feast.

3. RESTORATION

This leads immediately to the second parable in the text. It's about that fellow the king spots among the guests who isn't properly dressed for the occasion. A few weeks ago my wife and I received an invitation to a banquet for an institution we help support. At the bottom of the invitation were the letters RSVP, by which we were reminded to let the hosts know if

135

we would be coming or not. But below those typical letters was yet another note, one I don't often see. It read, "Black tie optional." In other words, this was to be a formal event. Preferably, ladies would attend in evening gowns, and gentlemen in tuxedoes. The fact the word "optional" appeared meant nothing! It was clear what was intended. I have no problem with this kind of expectation, even though we could not attend, nor do we have the formal attire it would have required. It seems to me that there ought to be occasions in life when we get dressed up. I was in the workforce, as most of you were, when the daily business suit began to be replaced with what was known originally as Casual Friday. Soon Casual Friday extended to every other day of the week for most employees. I remember when the phrase "Sunday clothes" really meant something. This was understood to be the best attire we have, whether overalls or suit, because it was a sign of our respect for the Lord's house. Today, of course, those ideas are completely passe in our society. Perhaps that's as it should be. Clearly the Lord doesn't require us to wear certain kinds of clothes to worship! So what does this parable mean, then?

If you'll indulge me, I want to offer a suggestion. The man in the story who did not have on the proper wedding garment was one of the good guys. What?! Now you remember at the end of the previous parable the good and the bad were invited into the feast. So I'm thinking the guests were there together, good and bad, or shall we say, those who thought themselves good, and who had no need of special raiment to come before the king. They had all they needed, their clothes were perfectly acceptable in their own eyes. But the bad – let's interpret them to be people who knew they didn't quite measure up, who saw their clothing as rags in comparison with what might be appropriate for the king's court -- these were people who, you might say, got a hand-out at the door. They were issued nicer clothes. And the man the king dressed down, thought his clothes were just fine, thank you very much.

The scene puts me in mind of the new recruit in basic training standing rod-stiff before the drill sergeant. Boots are shined, brass polished. But unknown to the young soldier, his handkerchief is sticking out of the back pocket. "You're out of uniform!" barks the sergeant. "No, sergeant, I mean, I've polished and spit shined and pressed and…" But the sergeant is not appeased. He launches into a tirade about what is appropriate and what is not. And the recruit, who thought he or she was all dressed up, experiences a classic dressing down.

It is possible for us to try to come into the presence of the Lord with only our own clothes, spiritually speaking. We can trust our own rightness before the Lord, our own capacity to do the right thing, to be the good guys. If we decide to come to the feast dressed that way, we are in for a rude awakening. For it is essential that we be properly dressed for our audience with the King. We must be clothed upon with Christ. [Galatians 3:27; Romans 13:14; Ephesians 4:24] "Dressed in his righteousness alone, faultless to stand before the throne." [Edward Mote, "The Solid Rock"]

This, then, is the restoration part of the story. For in our own righteousness, we discover ourselves to be like the Psalmist who said, 'If thou shoulds't mark iniquities, Lord, who could stand?' [Psalm 130:3] We are like Peter in the fishing boat who cried, 'Depart from me, Lord, for I am a sinner!' [Luke 5:8] But our Savior came not to call the righteous, but sinners, and it was while we were yet sinners that Christ died for us. [Matthew 9:13; Romans 5:8]

The invitation goes out to many, indeed to the whole world. But only those who come to Christ, and who thus are clothed with his righteousness, are chosen. Chosen not for who we are, but for who he is. To avoid an unpleasant dressing down, we dress up with the clothes he gives us!

THE GOOD SHEPHERD (AGAIN)

I am the good shepherd. The good shepherd lays down his life for the sheep... So there will be one flock, one shepherd. John 10:11, 16

One day last week a "Jeopardy!" clue concerned a book of the Bible that features light in the darkness, Lazarus and the Good Shepherd. The first contestant buzzed in with the response, "What is the book of Exodus?" That, of course, was incorrect. The second player then chimed in to ask, "What is Acts?" Also, wrong. The third player – the returning champion, by the way – made no attempt at the answer. The response guest host Anderson Cooper was looking for was the Gospel of John. Probably any of us would have known that, and it mystified me that these highly intelligent people, who know so much more about most things than I do, did not know this. Ask them anything about nearly anything and they could give you chapter and verse. But ask them a fairly simple question from the Bible and they're stumped! This wasn't the only clue they missed from the Bible category. Now it's true that sometimes the show's contestants are whizzes on Bible questions, but all too often these days there is an apparent lack of familiarity with basic biblical material that would not have been the case a couple of generations ago.

It is alarming to me that the beauty, truth and power of Scripture that we in the Christian community hold so dear is largely unknown to multitudes in our society today. I attribute that to the growing numbers of folks in our country demographers refer to as "Nones." That means, when polled about their religious affiliation, they would reply, "None." Some of our mission fields are very close to home, aren't they?

Surely one of the most familiar and beloved images in the Bible is Christ as the good shepherd. It comes to us, as the "Jeopardy!" clue evoked, from the Gospel of John. What a coincidence it is that our unison Scripture reading in worship last Sunday morning was the same passage that is the recommended Gospel lesson from the lectionary for today! The Good Shepherd again!

When Jesus referred to himself as the good shepherd, he was taking up a thread of spiritual truth found in the sacred writings we know as the Old Testament. This notion of the Lord as shepherd is a metaphor often used in Scripture. We think, for instance, of the beloved opening sentence of the Twenty-Third Psalm: "The Lord is my shepherd, I shall not want."

By the way, the other evening I watched an inspiring conversation between the U2 frontman Bono and the Bible translator Eugene Peterson whose work, The Message, has contemporized and simplified the language

138

of the Bible for today's readers. In that talk Dr. Peterson said that as a young lad he didn't always understand what the Bible meant when, for example, it referred to the Lord as a "rock," or a "strong tower." But as he studied the Psalms especially, he gradually came to realize what a metaphor was before he ever knew the word! Bono agreed, noting that when he was growing up in Ireland one of his favorite church songs was "The Lord's My Shepherd' -- and then he proceeded to sing it on the spot from memory and without accompaniment! There are wonderful metaphors in Scripture that seek to illustrate deep spiritual truth. The Lord as our shepherd is one.

The prophet Ezekiel, under the Lord's inspiration, criticized those who were supposed to be spiritual shepherds of the people of Israel because they were interested only in personal gain rather than the spiritual wellbeing of the people. "For thus says the Lord God: I myself will search for my sheep, and will seek them out... I will rescue them from all the places they have been scattered... I myself will be the shepherd of my sheep..." [Ezekiel 34:11, 12, 15] In the same vein the prophet Jeremiah cried, "Woe to the shepherds who destroy and scatter the sheep of my pasture! says the Lord... I myself will gather the remnant of my flock... and bring them back to their fold." [Jeremiah 23:1, 3] Ecclesiastes avers the sayings of the wise are 'given by one shepherd.' [Ecclesiastes 12:11] Isaiah, foretelling the coming Messiah, said: "He will feed his flock like a shepherd; he will gather the lambs in his arms." [Isaiah 40:11] And again the psalmist affirms we are the people of God's pasture, the sheep of his hand. [Psalm 95:7]

Hearing these references from the Hebrew Bible, we followers of Jesus can't help remembering the Gospel of Matthew's observation that 'when he saw the crowds he had compassion on them, for they were like sheep without a shepherd.' [Matthew 9:36] This comment, too, recalls Moses' prayer to God for a leader, "that the congregation of the Lord may not be like sheep without a shepherd." [Numbers 27:17]

There are other allusions to Christ as our shepherd in the New Testament besides this one from the Gospel of John. While we do not find a direct statement of Christ as the good shepherd in Luke's Gospel, what we do have there is the marvelous parable of the shepherd who leaves the ninety-nine sheep in the fold in order to search for – and find! -- the one that was missing. [Luke 15:3] Can there be any doubt as to who this figure of the searching shepherd represents? The Letter to the Hebrews draws to a close with a specific reference to the Lord Jesus as "the great shepherd of the sheep." [Hebrews 13:20] And the apostle Peter's readers were reminded: "you were going astray like sheep, but now you have returned to the shepherd and guardian of your souls" -- none other than Christ who "bore our sins in his body on the cross." [1 Peter 2:24, 25] It was Peter, you remember, who was commissioned by the Risen Jesus in that seaside encounter to "feed my sheep." [John 21:17]

In our passage today the Lord Jesus identified himself as the good shepherd. It's noteworthy that he used that particular adjective, "good", because on one occasion he insisted that no one but God is good! [Luke 18:19] In this passage he explained what the phrase "good shepherd" meant in several important ways. I have spoken from this text in this pulpit before, but this compelling subject cannot be emphasized enough. I invite you to think again with me about this unique portrait of the Good Shepherd.

1. THE GOOD SHEPHERD LAYS DOWN HIS LIFE FOR THE SHEEP

In the opening verses of John 10 our Lord introduces the discussion of shepherd and sheep with the illustration of the gatekeeper who opens the gate of the sheepfold for the shepherd who then calls his own sheep by name and they follow him out of the enclosure because they know his voice. [10:3-4] In the time of Christ few pastoral images were more familiar than shepherds and sheep. They could be seen in the countryside along the high plateaus that formed the backbone of the topography of Palestine, and they could be seen in the towns, where the sheep of several shepherds could be kept together in one sheepfold managed by the gatekeeper. To us, perhaps, one sheep looks about like any other. But to the trained eye of the shepherd, the one who had seen after them since they were lambs, the sheep were known individually. They depended on the shepherd for their security and nourishment, and the shepherd relied on them for his livelihood. So when he called them from the gate, they recognized his voice and came immediately to follow him out. The sheep of another flock paid no attention at all, for they would not recognize the voice of a stranger.

Years ago I read a story from a renowned preacher -- Arthur John Gossip --who told of serving as a chaplain on the front lines in Europe in the Great War. One early morning he heard a strange, high-pitched sound on the hill in no-man's-land. Looking through binoculars, he made out the form of a young boy walking over the hill with a small flock of sheep following him. Little did he know the danger he was in, of course, or maybe he did! But neither side of combatants wished to interrupt the youngster's work as he sang to the sheep and then passed out of sight. The sheep followed because they knew the voice of the shepherd. It became for Gossip a sign of peace in the midst of terrible war.

It was that kind of imagery that prepared Jesus' listeners for his powerful self-disclosure as the good shepherd, the one who would lay down his life for the sheep. There were others in that day who cared for sheep, hired hands who watched them in behalf of the shepherd. But while they performed a valuable service in the absence of the shepherd, they could not be trusted to risk their lives for the protection of the flock. The good shepherd, the one who truly is the shepherd, is ready to protect the sheep with his own life. This is the clear distinction between the good shepherd and those who care little for the flock. The good shepherd places himself between the flock and those that would destroy the sheep. Jesus was prepared to lay down his life for his sheep, and he did.

2. THE GOOD SHEPHERD KNOWS HIS OWN AND HIS KNOWN

Twice in this brief passage the Lord Jesus refers to himself as the good shepherd. In the first expression, as we've seen, he declares that the good shepherd lays down his life for the sheep, in distinction from the hired hand. [10:11] With the second use of the figure Jesus says, "I know my own and my own know me." [v. 14] This harks back to those earlier verses in the chapter where the shepherd calls and his sheep recognize his voice.

Does it matter to you that our Lord knows us so well? Some, I suspect, would prefer a little anonymity with regard to a relationship with God. It's a bit disconcerting to realize that Christ knows us, really knows us!

3. THE GOOD SHEPHERD BRINGS OTHER SHEEP

In this passage, too, is that striking comment that our Lord has other sheep that do not belong to this fold. It means, I expect, that our Savior's mission ultimately was not limited to the house of Israel, though it was to that fold he first came. He has other sheep. It's a way of speaking about the gospel that is for all people. In the years after Christ's crucifixion and resurrection his followers would carry the gospel message to the farthest reaches of the Roman Empire and beyond. Tradition has the apostle Thomas, for example, traveling to the Far East and suffering martyrdom there. Paul, feeling especially designated by the Risen Christ to bring the gospel to the Gentile world, dedicated himself to proclaiming the gospel where the name of Christ had never been heard before. [Romans 15:20] He wanted to go as far as Spain, but an appointment with Caesar interrupted those plans.

Today, the Lord is still gathering other sheep. But it is interesting that Christ does not speak of "other flocks." There is one flock, one Shepherd. [10:16] The Lord's followers come in all nationalities and races. But we are one flock. Within the great variety of Christ's church, there is a unity that only Christ assures and makes possible. He alone is our Good Shepherd.

FRIEND AT MIDNIGHT

… because of his persistence he will get up and give him whatever he needs. Luke 11:8

Have you ever wondered how the Lord keeps track of all the prayers that continually ascend to Heaven? We're reasonably sure there is no humongous mainframe computer system receiving, sorting and filing. And we are grateful that we never hear a recorded celestial message telling us that all angels are currently assisting other pray-ers! If for no other reason than the sheer magnitude of prayers, we are awestruck by the omniscience, the all-knowing-ness, of our God!

This has been reiterated for us by the groundswell of international prayers during the crisis in Ukraine. Even during the height of the pandemic we did not witness such an outpouring of prayer as we've seen on the news in recent days. And there is a surprising unanimity of perspective across political and national lines. Prayers for the cessation of the war, prayers for justice in response to the aggression by a superpower, prayers for the people of Ukraine suffering physical harm, displacement, economic woes, and the loss of access to daily necessities. Prayers for the Ukrainian military standing against overwhelming odds. Prayers for our military that, with allies, may be involved to some degree. Our own prayers have mingled with those of countless millions around the world.

Ukraine itself is an unusually religious nation, with over eighty percent of the population Eastern Orthodox Christian. A sizeable Jewish population lives there, along with those of other faiths. We are certain that all their prayers have risen without cessation since before the Russian invasion.

There are over two billion people who profess Christian faith out of a world population of almost eight billion – nearly a third of the people in the world are adherents of what still is the largest religion worldwide. We realize, of course, that not all of us are as faithful in prayer as we should be! Just for the sake of discussion, suppose just thirty percent of us do pray regularly, say once a day. If my arithmetic is right, that would be six hundred million prayers for the Lord to deal with daily! Some Christians pray much more frequently than that, and Scripture enjoins us to do so. Our prayers run the gamut of topics – not only for peace in the world, and easing of the pandemic, but also most often for the very personal concerns we all have for our loved ones, our health and safety, our nation and on and on. I confess that my own prayers tend to be quite repetitious and superficial. Sometimes I imagine the Lord sighing, 'Oh, it's that Estes guy again with the same old tune!' Yet we never have the sense that we must wait in line to pray. We may not always feel that our prayers are answered -- and we suspect that's due to our shortsightedness more than anything else – but we do typically believe they are heard by our loving and powerful God.

1. JESUS TAUGHT THE IMPORTANCE OF PRAYER

A primary reason for our confidence in prayer, as well as our continuing practice of it, is the teaching of the Lord Jesus. In word and example, Jesus taught the unequaled importance of prayer. Not only did he insist that his followers should pray to God, but he further made some astonishing claims regarding prayer. 'Whatever you ask in my name will be granted. Ask and you will receive,' and so on. [Cf., John 14:13; Matthew 7:7; Luke 11:9]

It's in the context of a conversation about prayer that Doctor Luke records the Lord's parable under consideration today. Jesus had been praying "in a certain place" when one of his disciples asked him to teach them to pray as John the Baptist had taught his own followers. This is where Luke's Gospel provides a brief version of the Lord's Prayer. Matthew's version is the one we usually recite. [Matthew 6:9-13] Luke's rendering of it is even more succinct, just three verses long. And immediately after sharing that prayer, Jesus told the story interpreters refer to as the Parable of the Importunate Friend. My term for it is the Friend at Midnight. The thrust of the parable, we may note, is the need for persistence in prayer. A parable usually has but one major point to make, and this seems to be it for this one, though we'll have a bit more to say about that in a moment.

It's not the only story Christ told like this. You remember the Parable of the Widow and the Unjust Judge in this connection. The widow in that story was so persistent that the hardnosed judge finally relented to grant her justice. [Cf. Luke18:1-8] By the way, that story and the one we're thinking of today are found only in the Gospel of Luke.

2. SOME CURIOUS THINGS IN THE PARABLE

There are some curious things about today's parable that our casual reading might not notice. For instance, Jesus specifically included the disciples in this story. "Which one of you," says one translation. [RSV] "Suppose you have a friend," says the NIV. The listener/reader is drawn immediately into the story.

Another interesting thing is that the one who is called "friend" is not the importunate or persistent one in the story, at least not initially. No, the person making the late night request is not the one termed friend, but rather the householder. The friend at midnight isn't the one who came knocking but the one who was asleep with his family, yet who came to the door, and ultimately responded to the need. We're reminded of the old proverb: 'A friend in need is a friend indeed.' It's not that the friend has a need, but the one who responds when <u>another</u> has a need, that's the friend. So in this parable.

There are actually three friends in the story. There's the homeowner, first. He might not have been happy about it, but he eventually did what he could to help. The one making the request is also a friend, we realize, because he wouldn't presume to call on the other person at such an hour if he were not on good terms. And the way the story begins indicates the two fellows were friends, maybe neighbors. There is also a third friend, though. He never actually appears in the story but is referenced by the one who came with a request. 'A friend of mine has arrived,' he said. It's a situation that undoubtedly happened with some regularity in ancient Palestine. People traveling from place to place had no way of letting others know their schedule, or when they might arrive for a visit. Lodgings were not easy to find if travelers got into town after dark. The best they could do was to locate the home of their friend or relative, knock on the door, and hope for the best. This traveling friend, given the rules of hospitality in that place and time, could not be refused. Certainly he would be welcomed into the home. The problem was, though, that there were insufficient extra provisions in the house to care for an unexpected guest. These were not people of wealth. They were ordinary folks living day to day, providing as best they could for their families with little to spare. Swallowing his pride, this first fellow would go to a neighbor and ask a favor. Incidentally, the word "persistence" in our text can also mean "shamelessly." Fearing the embarrassment of having nothing to offer his guest, the man went to his neighbor, accepting the embarrassment that went with that!

During the ice storm in our area a few weeks ago, thousands of people were without power for an extended time -- days or weeks. One couple of our acquaintance lost power late one night. They are young and in good health, so ordinarily they would have handled the situation on their own. But they had just brought home from the hospital preemie twins who were quite susceptible to illness. The new mom and dad were frantic as to how to keep them safe. They called a friend, a member of their church, who lived fairly close by and asked if they could bring the babies over for the night. Without hesitation Noah said, "Yes, absolutely, come right now!" They did, and everyone made it through the night. And for a couple days more, they prevailed on the good-heartedness of their friend. When I heard this, I immediately thought of this parable Jesus told. The difference, though, is that in the story the householder seemed reluctant to be disturbed. Not so Noah. He welcomed PJ and Matt and their little girls with open arms. "Stay as long as you need to," he said. "If we lose power here,

145

we'll figure something else out!" That's a friend at midnight, don't you think?

The way the Lord Jesus told the story indicates that the neighbor felt a bit put-upon, and perhaps we can understand why. His family was sleeping and he didn't want them disturbed. Couldn't this wait till morning? And three loaves of bread? Who needs that much? Even if the loaves were not what we think of today, it sounds like a sizeable request. Maybe the neighbor suspected the bread wasn't just for that visitor! This pushed the limits of friendship, and Jesus noted that. So it wasn't for friendship alone that the householder finally came through. The way Jesus says it, it was because of the man's persistence. Maybe he kept on knocking at the door. The story doesn't tell us. But there was something about the request that could not be ignored.

3. PERSEVERENCE IN PRAYER

Now again, a parable is meant to highlight a particular spiritual truth. We realize that the Lord Jesus was not implying that our heavenly Father doesn't like to be disturbed with our requests, or that in any way God is reluctant to come to our aid. The attitude of the householder is almost exactly opposite of what we know Jesus taught about God. 'If you, being evil, know how to give good gifts to your children,' said Jesus, 'how much more does your heavenly Father give good gifts to you?' [Matthew 7:11; Luke 11:13] God is more eager to grant our needs than we are to even ask! Yet our requests are to be made in the name of Christ and in accordance with the will of God, not our own will. So the reluctance of the householder is not a description of God at all. The story focuses on the persistence of the one making the request. Or perhaps a better way of understanding it is the notion of perseverance! Jesus is inviting his followers to faithfully persevere in their prayer life, not because our God is forgetful of our concerns, but because we ourselves tend to lose heart and to settle for weak faith.

Perseverance in prayer suggests living in the hope of the graciousness of God. It means we trust, even when times are difficult, and especially then. May our confidence and assurance in prayer be strengthened as we approach the Table of our Lord once more.

THE GARDENER

He replied, 'Sir, let it alone for one more year, until I dig around it...' Luke 13:8

Some folks have a green thumb when it comes to caring for flowers, shrubs and gardens. That's not one of my gifts. Now for pruning and discarding, I'm world class, but that's another matter. My lack of skill as a plant grower is a source of concern as I read the Bible. For again and again God's people are urged to produce good fruit. We realize, of course, that this is not so much a reference to veggies and flora, but to a spiritual fruitfulness. This is small comfort when I consider how ineffective my own fruit-bearing has been in that regard also! So when we come to our Lord's parable in today's Scripture passage, it's a little unsettling.

It's a story about a fig tree that for some reason did not yield fruit. Fig trees were common in Jesus' day and people enjoyed eating figs. They had been a staple of human diet from time immemorial. Fig leaves were fashioned as the first human clothing, according to Genesis 3:7! Many still enjoy figs today. In my youth there was a chewy treat called Fig Newtons. I haven't seen those for a while, but I expect they're still around. They weren't my favorite, but they were popular among young people back in the day. A friend of ours recently gave us a jar of fig jam she made from the fruit of a tree in her yard, the first I'd ever had.

1. AN OPEN-ENDED STORY

Fig trees or shrubs are, as I understand it, fairly easy to grow and care for. Actually, the fig is not a fruit strictly speaking, but a kind of inverted flower. Fig trees thrive best in climates of long, hot summers, so Palestine was a good place for them. People who know about fig trees say it takes three to five years for a new one to start producing fruit. In the Lord's parable the owner of the vineyard where a fig tree was planted came looking for figs on it but found none. Three years had passed, but there were no figs. He called his gardener over and told him to cut it down. 'No sense it taking up valuable space, using up the soil!' But the gardener thought there was a chance the tree could produce. It needed work, and he would do it. 'Let me work with it another year,' he said, 'and if it still doesn't produce, it can be cut down.'

That's where the story ends. Wouldn't you like to know what happened? Did the cultivating and fertilizing have a good effect? Did the tree produce figs? Or was it just wasted effort? Jesus doesn't tell us. He left the story open-ended. It is as if he was saying the jury is still out as to

147

whether or not the tree would produce good fruit. That's where we come in. Because we, like those who first heard Jesus' story, recognize that it's not about fig trees at all.

Luke is the only Gospel writer to include this parable. But there is a story in Matthew and Mark that comes to mind in this connection. It's that chilling narrative from the last week of Jesus' earthly life when he was returning to the city of Jerusalem from his overnight stay in Bethany. And he saw a fig tree by the side of the road. We're told he was hungry, so he went over to the tree to pick some figs. But the tree had nothing on it but leaves! No fruit. "May no fruit ever come from you again!" he said. And the tree immediately withered. The disciples were shocked. But the Lord then said that if they had faith, they could even move mountains. [Matthew 21:18-22; Mark 11:14] This story seems so out of character with the Jesus we know! But what if Jesus' was using that fig tree in the same way he was telling this parable? Was he making a larger point? If so, what was it?

Israel had enjoyed a special calling from the Lord, had received the patriarchal covenant, been granted the divine Law through Moses, stood for the heritage of faith in the one Almighty God. Yet its history was marked by vacillation between faithfulness to God and waywardness in pursuit of other deities and values. Prophetic warnings had called the people back to the Lord, but instead of regarding itself as the Lord's servant, Israel presumed on its favored status as God's chosen people. Rather than representing the Lord's way as a light to the nations, they huddled in exclusivity. Instead of living the Law of God in genuine freedom, they became enslaved to a rigid set of regulations that were imposed on top of that Law in the effort to earn God's blessing. The Lord had exercised great restraint in dealing with the people, though there were periods of severe hardship such as the Babylonian exile and the loss of national independence by a succession of foreign conquerors. The parable Jesus told -- and the withering of the fig tree -- illustrates the dire spiritual condition not only of Israel, but the whole world when the Messiah Jesus came.

2. THE GARDENER IS AN INTRIGUING CHARACTER

The gardener in Christ's parable is an intriguing character. He served at the pleasure of the vineyard owner, but when the order was given to cut down the non-bearing tree, the gardener bravely countered with a different suggestion. Clearly the relationship between the owner and the gardener was one of mutual trust. Otherwise the gardener would not have taken it upon himself to challenge the initial order, nor would the landowner have listened to the suggestion. We hear the gardener say, 'Sir, let it alone for one more year.' He offers to dig around the tree, to fertilize it, care for it in a special way. We cannot keep from comparing this gardener with the role of Jesus himself, can we?

Jesus came into the world, the ultimate expression of divine love and forbearance, 'not to condemn the world, but that the world through him might be saved.' [John 3:17] He did not have to persuade the Heavenly Father to do this, for it was in God's redemptive plan from before creation. [Ephesians 1:4] God's love for the world was the motivation for sending Jesus, the only begotten Son, to save us.

Consider, too, the work of the Lord Jesus. His ministry was exercised not from the tower at the edge of the vineyard, but down in the dirt and manure of the daily grind. He poured out his sweat and blood to nurture that failing tree. And the result seemed hopeless! It cost him his life! Yet in giving himself, the buds of new life began to show themselves as he, in victory over death, continued to work the plant and, by his Spirit, nurture it into bearing fruit. We today are in that period of nurturing at the hand of the divine Gardener. It is a time of testing, of trial and error, of growth and grafting, of loss and decay. In each generation the jury is still out as to whether genuine fruit of repentance and grace will prevail over our tendency toward complacency and self-centeredness.

There is in the parable, then, an implication of judgment. 'If it bears fruit, well and good. If not, you can cut it down.' I'm not sure we can sense the catch in the gardener's throat in saying this. He loves the tree, sees its potential, wants to do whatever it takes to save it, but in the end, it will either bear fruit or it will not. This is the inevitable test not only of the tree in the story, but of our faithfulness to God's call in our own lives and time. Jesus once voiced the concern that 'when the Son of Man returns, will he find faith on earth?' [Luke 18:8] That question comes right at the end of another parable unique to Luke, the story of the widow and unjust judge we have mentioned before.

3. IS THERE A CONTEMPORARY CONNECTION?

We tune in to this parable from our Lord at a time of international crisis. We have watched in horror as Russia unleashed its great military might against a neighbor nation that has much less capacity to withstand the onslaught. We have heard the cries of the wounded, the separated, the bereaved. We have walked with television journalists through the rubble of fine cities. We have heard the plea to our own Congress from the president of Ukraine. We have sensed the tension among nearby nations, and even in our own. The threat to world peace is real. How can we be concerned with this ancient Bible passage when there is so much at stake? Is our worship just a means of sticking our head in the sand. Are our prayers only a way of hoping for the best? Today's complex geopolitical situation may cause us to wonder if our story from Scripture has anything to teach us about the perils of modern life in a nuclear age. These questions challenge us, but they must be met head-on. For the affirmation of our Christian faith is that it is truth and life for all times and all peoples. What then shall we say to these things?

We may say, first, that the parable reminds us that God, our God, is sovereign. It is God's vineyard, God's fig tree, God's world. God knows where there is genuine fruitfulness in service to his redemptive will and where there is resistance to his purposes. The darkness of this world may dim our realization of God's power and authority, but that does not limit God's divine will. We must rebuke the voices of our distrust and acknowledge anew that God is working his purposes out. We don't forget the context of the parable, either, where the Lord addressed Pilate's heinous act of mingling the Galileans' blood with their sacrifices to God, and the tragic collapse of a tower in Jerusalem that killed eighteen people. It was a harsh world then, too. The parable and its preface call us all to sober repentance and reflection on the urgency of it.

In the second place we remember that our Savior, the Master Gardener, has come with the intent of making right that which is so wrong with the world. Christ came into the world to effect reconciliation between humanity and God, and between peoples. In Christ, the dividing walls have been brought down. [Ephesians 2:14] Jesus Christ is our peace. His labor is not in vain. He has done what he set out to do, making possible not only our own individual salvation but ultimately restoring the world to harmony with God in God's own time. The forces of evil cannot prevail against the divine love that Jesus Christ has brought. For 'in him was life and the life was the light of all people.' [John 1:4] Our responsibility and our joy is to proclaim the victory in Christ, to lift him up that all may come to him. [John 12:32]

So in the parable we see the patience and work of our Savior, but we see that there is also a reckoning to come. We his followers are held accountable for our faithfulness to his will and way. And indeed all persons are to one day stand before the judgment seat of God. [2 Corinthians 5:10] We who belong to Christ will be dressed in his righteousness, not our own. Those who choose not to receive him, though, will face a divine judgment resulting from their rebellious refusal. Nations, not just individuals, will bow before the Lord. [Psalm 86:9] So the issue the parable raises for us, even in the face of international strife, is the depth of our own commitment to see the hand of the Master Gardener at work and to trust his matchless care for the world he came to save.

NO FAIR!

For the kingdom of heaven is like a landowner who went out early in the morning to hire laborers for his vineyard. Matthew 20:1-16

"My thoughts are not your thoughts, neither are your ways my ways," says the Lord in Scripture. [Isaiah 55:8] Nowhere is that truth more evident than in the parables of Jesus. In the world of the parables, conventional wisdom is turned on its ear, the foregone conclusion is bypassed. Of course we don't quite sense the surprise in these stories any more because we have heard them so often. But we have no trouble believing that Christ's first hearers were certainly surprised, if not shocked, when he told them. The stories were so astonishing, and so counter-intuitive, that they were faithfully preserved through untold generations of hand-copied manuscripts, and they have even withstood the printing press, the computer, and the plethora of Bible translations available today. Most of the parables are quite brief, just a few verses. Notable exceptions are the stories of the Good Samaritan, the Prodigal Son, Lazarus and the Rich Man, and even the parable under consideration this morning, sometimes referred to as the Parable of Hours. Still, it is just sixteen verses long. Yet it remains one of the most challenging parables for expositors, simple in its presentation but difficult in its interpretation.

The parables of Jesus are packed with human pathos. There's always something in them we can identify with, something of the human condition itself, and often something that surprises, mystifies and even disturbs us. That is the case with today's story, too. The situation was one the Lord Jesus must have witnessed many times in his hometown of Nazareth. Some of us may have seen this sort of thing in our own day as well. In the pre-dawn twilight, the town square was a gathering place for people who hoped to be hired for a day's work, at least. Landowners, employers, would go there to find workers to supplement their usual workforce, especially in peak seasons of planting and harvesting. Life was not easy for these would-be workers, and much depended on their getting the nod from a manager or boss. A day's wage could mean the difference between putting food on the table for the family, or not. That they did not have ongoing, regular employment suggests their circumstances were extreme. Nothing is said about their skill level, their age, or fitness for work. It is assumed they were ready, able and eager to go into the vineyard.

Those who were hired early that morning were counting their blessings! They happily agreed to work for the typical day's wage – a denarius -- and headed out to the vineyard. Three hours later the landowner returned to the market square and hired more workers. But in this instance he said only, 'I'll pay you what is right.' Satisfied with the word of the landowner, they immediately went to work. Throughout the day the scene was repeated, at noon, and at three, and finally about five, or just an hour or so before sundown. It's a wonder there were still men hoping for work that late in the day, but there they were. Evidently the vintner was surprised too. He asked, "Why have you been standing here all day long doing nothing?" And the answer they gave was the heartbreaking reality of so many, even today: "Because no one has hired us."

The unemployment rate in the United States last month was 4.4%, over seven million people. Despite the gradual economic recovery from the recession of the last decade, there are still multitudes of people who cannot find work, and many of those who do are among the under-employed with part-time wages and no benefits. So this parable brings to light the predicament of people who are jobless, and it takes little reading between the lines to hear the desperation in the reply of the last workers in the parable.

To this point the story may have been mildly interesting to our Lord's first audience, but they were all quite familiar with the hiring practices of the few and the need for jobs among the many. They might have quibbled with the landowner's continuous returning to the market for workers, thinking that any agribusinessman would know how many people he would need on any given day. But otherwise they would have felt comfortable with the progression of the tale, maybe even bored. But suddenly things changed.

1. CONSTERNATION

As the sun went down the workers picked up their tools and began to walk back to the steward's hut where they would receive their pay. Nowadays most employees are paid by the week or the month, but occasionally still there are day-laborers. For the temps in the story who had no promise of a job tomorrow, the pay at the end of the workday was crucial. But as the men are assembling in the gathering darkness, they notice the vineyard owner speaking to his steward. Christ gives only a hint as to the nature of the conversation between the landowner and his steward, but it must have been fascinating! The owner told his trusted manager what he wanted to do: 'Give everyone the full day's wage, regardless. Oh, and by the way, begin with the last first.' The steward might have raised an eyebrow in surprise, might even have asked for further clarification, depending on their relationship. Did he take the part of the earliest workers, or did he rejoice in the decision regarding the later ones? We have no way of knowing. But at once the steward made the announcement that those who were hired last would be the first to be paid, and then progressively to those who had been hired first. This detail must have sounded unusual to Christ's hearers, but not a big concern. Those who had worked all day were, no doubt, ready to go home, but a few more minutes wouldn't make much difference. Then they saw that the men hired for only one hour of work were paid a denarius, the full day's wage!

At this Christ's hearers must have perked up. What kind of employer does that? And if he is so generous with these latest hires, how much more will he give to those who have worked much longer in the vineyard? Christ anticipates this response and indicates that indeed those who had been hired earlier in the day were fully expecting a greater paycheck. But they were crestfallen when the steward handed them also a single denarius apiece!

As youngsters on the school playground, you and I were well aware of the unwritten rules of the games we played. And if one of our group ignored those rules to his or her own advantage, we would cry out, "No fair!" Children seem to have an innate sense of what is fair and unfair, don't they? That expectation of fair play goes with us into adulthood, too, and most of us have had experiences in life evoking a cry of "No fair!" Either we didn't get what we felt we deserved, or what we got was much less desirable than what we were led to expect.

The workers in Christ's story who were among the first to go into the vineyard, once they realized they were to receive the same pay as those who worked least, began to grumble against the landowner. You can almost hear the hoarse whispers of those weary men: 'It's not fair!'

We expect some in Christ's audience were muttering the same phrase! And truth be told, it goes against our grain a little, too. It just doesn't seem right, and we find ourselves in a state of consternation. It's all well and good for the vineyard guy to pay whatever he likes to those who worked so little, but surely he's prepared to reward those hard-working first hires accordingly!

The landowner can't help hearing the complaints in the ranks. Maybe the steward was getting the brunt of the argument when the owner stepped in, reminding those who had been in the field all day that they themselves agreed to the wages in advance. They were not being shorted or slighted or mistreated. The verbal contract was being honored. No bonus had been hinted at. Likewise the others who worked various lengths of time during the day received no more or less than was promised. The landowner had simply told them, 'I will pay you what is right.' And he did.

There is another shade of red in this tapestry. Those workers hired first put it to the landowner this way: 'You have made them equal to us!' They had reason to believe that their faithfulness throughout the day would grant them a place of privilege in the eyes of the owner, and now he seems to have degraded them to the level of, well, these shiftless one-hour workers!

Those who first heard Jesus tell this story could not miss the fact that he wasn't just talking about vineyards and owners and laborers. They realized, as indeed we do, that he was saying something about God's dealings with humanity. And that causes us even more concern. Is the Lord of the universe unfair? Will he not reward those who have been most faithful more than those who have come so late to his service?

2. CONSOLATION

Yes, there is a bit of consternation in this parable, not only in the attitude of those workers hired first, but also in our own as we read the story. But upon further reflection, you and I may also notice consolation. We can, for instance, empathize with those late-afternoon workers who had waited all the long day for someone to hire them, and just when it seemed another sun would set on their unrelieved misery, the landowner came one more time to the square. And the rest, as we say, is history. We can imagine the jubilant conversation as one of those laborers came through the door that evening. "Honey, I'm home! You'll never guess what happened!" And then he produced the coin and told the amazing story. He couldn't believe his good fortune. Of course he had worked hard before the sun went down, but he knew he didn't really deserve the full day's pay. He couldn't have quarreled with a tenth of that. That joy was replicated in the households of all those one-hour workers. What a difference this would make for those families. Food on the table. Clothes for the kids starting school. Something needed for the house. There is unexpected blessing in this parable. We could call it grace.

3. CONFLUENCE

The story echoes some other parables of the Lord, a confluence of teaching. You can detect something of the same lesson in the Parable of the Prodigal Son. The father goes head-over-heels to welcome the wayward boy back, despite the grumbling older brother. You can hear a similar teaching in the Parable of the Wedding Banquet where those who were often overlooked in society – the poor, the disabled – were brought into the feast, because the favored first invitees sent their regrets. Maybe you can pick up a similar thought in the story of the Good Samaritan. Out of his own resources he paid for the care of a beaten man who on a normal day wouldn't have given him the time of day. And we remember that the prayer of the sinful publican in the temple was heard rather than the prayer of the Pharisee who was so impressed with his own righteousness. In Christ's stories about the kingdom of God, there's a different kind of fairness going on, an entirely different ordering of things. The last and the least are first.

In today's parable, as in some others, those least deserving receive grace. It's a reminder that salvation is a gift. It's not earned no matter how hard we may work at it. Divine mercy is not dependent on our doing and being good. It is dependent on God's being good! Grace happens, and yes, even to us.

I don't believe this story offers a modern economic theory that could turn the bad news of unemployment around today. We do note, however, that many corporate execs are raking in unprecedented salaries at a time when the 'little man' is struggling to make ends meet. Contrast that with the compassion and generosity of the landowner in Christ's parable. You have to wonder which attitude displays genuine fairness.

If we find our sense of justice and fairness challenged in this story, and we are a bit unnerved by it, there is at the same time an Aha! moment. It lifts the invisible curtain to reveal a magnificently merciful God who welcomes even the likes of us into the vineyard, both early and late, granting us salvation far beyond what we could ever deserve.

LAZARUS (THE PARABLE)

There was a rich man who was dressed in purple and fine linen and who feasted sumptuously every day. And at his gate lay a poor man named Lazarus, covered with sores... Luke 16:19-20

Years ago I heard an old gospel song that was inspired by the parable under consideration today. You may have heard it as well. It begins like this:

> Only a tramp was Lazarus that day;
> He lay down by the rich man's gate.
> He begged for crumbs from the rich man to eat,
> But they left him to die like a tramp on the street.
>
> He was some mother's darling, he was some mother's son.
> Once he was fair and once he was young.
> Some mother, she rocked him, her little darling to sleep.
> But they left him to die like a tramp on the street.
> [Grady and Hazel Cole, 1940]

The song's haunting melody and message was recorded by many artists, people as different as Hank Williams, Sr., and Joan Baez. The song doesn't confine itself to the actual story that Jesus told, but it captures the desolate circumstances of the one Jesus called Lazarus.

1. NAMES IN THE BIBLE

Names are important in the Bible. Often biblical names have a significance that today's names do not. For instance, Jacob, the younger twin brother of Esau, was so named because he came from the womb holding onto his brother's foot. [Genesis 25:26] The name means "supplanter" – not all that complimentary. But as a young man Jacob would show he was appropriately named. He fooled his aging father into thinking he was his brother, and he took advantage of Esau to claim the birthright that should have gone to the eldest. But after wrestling with the angel of the Lord years later, God changed his name to Israel, which meant "one who struggles with God." [Genesis 32:28] Thomas, one of the Lord's disciples, was also a twin who was called Didymus. [John 11:16] Both names mean "twin." Thomas is Aramaic and Didymus is Greek. Jesus changed Simon's name to Peter, or Cephas, the rock. [John 1:42] Saul of Tarsus became known as Paul, a Greek version of the name, when he embarked on his mission to the Gentile world. We have noticed also the importance of the name Emmanuel – "God with us" – ascribed to Christ, and the name Jesus means "God saves." So names often mean something in the Bible.

So it's interesting that of the fifty or so parables of Jesus, only one includes a proper name! It's this one that features a poor man named Lazarus. On the strength of what we've said so far, you may be thinking, 'Well, Lazarus must mean something.' And you're right! The word Lazarus is the Greek form of the Hebrew name Eleazar, which meant "one whom God has helped." That seems especially apt, since in the story Lazarus got little help from anybody else! I've inserted the parenthetical description in the title of this sermon as a way of differentiating this person from another man named Lazarus. He was, as you know, the person Jesus raised from death. He lived in the village of Bethany near Jerusalem, was a brother of Martha and Mary, the family that has the distinction of being referred to as "loved" by Jesus. [John 11:5] Lazarus was not an uncommon name in those days. The parable we focus on today, though, is not about that man from Bethany, but about another Lazarus, a person whose name meant something!

There is another proper name in the story, too. It's Abraham, the great patriarch, whose own name God changed from Abram because he was to be 'the father of many nations.' [Genesis 17:5] In the parable Abraham is a figure not unlike the way we may think of St. Peter at the golden gate! He clearly is God's representative, receiving the poor man into his loving arms in heaven. There is, though, a conversation between Father Abraham and the rich man, who also has died but is now in Hades, a place of torment. That character in the parable has no name, though the tradition in the church has called him "Dives," a word the Latin Vulgate Bible translates as "rich."

There is, then, in this story a rare portrayal of the afterlife, centering on three personalities: the poor man Lazarus, the rich man, and Abraham. We realize that here as in all the parables, Christ used figurative language to offer spiritual truth. It isn't a full description of heaven or hell. But the depiction nevertheless grants us the realization that there is a life beyond this one, and that there is judgment there.

2. JUSTICE – A REVERSAL OF VALUES

Or perhaps a better word is "justice." For in Bible times justice was scarce, especially for those with little or no means. Jesus was particularly sensitive to the plight of the defenseless and those who had no advocate with the authorities. Thus he told the story of the widow who had been wronged, taking her case before an unjust (and uncaring) judge. [Luke 18:1ff] It was her persistence alone that persuaded the judge to grant her justice. Rulers and others in authority in those days placed little value on human life, still less in the rightful claims of their subjects unless there was something in it for themselves. Yet even if justice was illusive in the realities of this life, Jesus here and elsewhere shows that there is divine justice in the life to come.

The Lord actually gave us few details of the lives of Lazarus and the rich man. We are not told, for instance, that Lazarus was especially devout, or that he lived an exemplary life that resulted in his reception by Abraham. He was impoverished and ill, and these difficulties had left him at the rich man's gate. On the other hand, we have no indication in the story that the rich man was especially wicked, or that his wealth had been gained by underhanded dealings. Perhaps he could have been more responsive to the beggar at this door, providing something more than crumbs, though at least he didn't have his people drive the man away. But what we do know is that in his earthly life Lazarus was miserable, while Dives was privileged. But after death this situation was reversed.

It is challenging to notice that the torment of the rich man did not seem to arise from terrible deeds, gross immorality, or any of the wrongdoings we usually associate with such a fate. It was for indifference. This man who could have made a difference for good did not. He knew Lazarus, but he had not seen him, not really.

But when he looked up from Hades, he recognized Lazarus beside Abraham. He asked Abraham to send Lazarus to dip his finger in water and let a drop fall on the rich man's tongue! Lazarus had begged for crumbs. Now Dives begs for a drop of water! In this story as in other teachings, our Lord insists: "the last shall be first, and the first last." There is in the kingdom of God a reversal of values from the way the world operates. And though justice may elude the weak and disenfranchised now, there is a divine imprint of right and wrong that will not be denied. The arc of history is long, it has been said, but it inclines toward justice. (Martin Luther King)

Our Lord's parable of the rich man and Lazarus is one of the most disturbing verbal portrayals in Scripture. Inevitably it reminds us of our own failure to acknowledge the needs of others, warning that a life of ease, oblivious to the evident suffering around us, will find the balance shifted in the life to come. Most of us have felt genuinely guilty at some point because we did not help another person, even though we had the means to do so. There are all kinds of reasons and justifications for our inaction, most of them quite plausible to us. But the sensitive person retains a lingering concern that more should have been done.

Invariably, also, the story raises our defenses. There are many people, we realize, who want to take advantage of the generosity and hospitality of others. We know, too, that our resources are limited, and we can't respond to every need. Our primary responsibility, we are convinced, must be to our nearest and dearest – and all too often we feel sadly unable to respond even to those needs as we'd like.

On the other hand, we also have had the experience of trying to be helpful, only to end up making matters worse, or to cause misunderstanding. Sometimes we've reached into our pocket not out of a sense of concern for the individual, but from a desire to brush that person off, or even a fear of what they might do if we fail to help. Often we are content with a band-aid approach to needs rather than becoming fully involved with the person or family to determine root causes and struggle with long-term solutions. Who has time for that?

At some level, too, many of us can identify with the poor man in the parable, the one beaten down by life. We may not have met the direst of circumstances as he did, but we have known something of the pain of not having what we need when needed, of falling short of our own expectations, of experiencing hurt and loneliness through no fault of our own. So this story evokes a range of feelings, many of which are quite uncomfortable. And the next part of the parable doesn't make things any better!

Abraham's answer to the rich man is chilling. "Son, remember…" The rich man – part of the Abrahamic family, after all -- is urged to remember the wealth and privilege he had so taken for granted, to remember his own carelessness about those far less fortunate. And then Abraham observes that a great chasm has been fixed been heaven and Hades, and there can be no crossing between them.

The tormented man suddenly finds a concern for his own brothers who have survived him. 'Let Lazarus go warn my five brothers to mend their ways.' But no! Even this is denied him. Again Abraham's words are telling, indicating that there is plenty of warning in the Scriptures for those who will heed them. But since they ignore those warnings, they wouldn't be convinced to repent even if someone came back from the dead!

3. ANOTHER FIGURE

Suddenly the story has a different sense, does it not? Instead of just the hapless Lazarus or the careless Dives, we seemingly see another figure in the story. That old gospel song I mentioned picked up on it, not being limited to the story itself. So it continues like this:

> Jesus who died on Calvary's tree,
> Shed his life's blood for you and for me;
> They pierced his side, his hands and his feet,
> And they left him to die like a tramp on the street.

159

He was Mary's own darling, he was Mary's own Son;
Once he was fair and once he was young.
And Mary, she'd rocked him, her little darling to sleep;
But they left him to die like a tramp on the street.

The song detects that there is something beyond the parable that it is pointing to. Isn't there One who has in fact risen from death? And isn't it the case that many still reject that fact and its implications? But the song also knows that this One, Mary's own Son, has taken our place. From our poverty of spirit to our arrogant indifference, Jesus Christ has taken our place. He bled and died for you and for me! Understood this way, there is not only judgment in this story, but also grace. For though he died on Calvary's tree, he was gloriously raised to grant life to all who will trust in him! Here the emotions of the parable are reduced and the Person who tells it stands forth as the One who has bridged the great chasm fixed between heaven and Hades. He takes our guilt upon himself, he takes our weakness in his strength, he receives us into his family.